The Heart of Tracking

THE HEART

of

TRACKING

Inner and Outer Practices
of Nature Awareness

Essays by

RICHARD VACHA

Illustrated by

KAYTA PLESCIA

MOUNT VISION PRESS

INVERNESS, CALIFORNIA

MOUNT VISION PRESS
Inverness, California

MVP 002

ISBN 978-0-9962467-5-0
Printed in the United States of America
First Printing

I dedicate this book to my vision for a global ban on predator hunting.

CONTENTS

The Heart of Tracking

Introduction

Tracking, at its surface, is simply the art of identifying animals by their footprints. But if you scratch this surface, tracking will take you on a journey deep into the heart of nature and into your own heart as well. It will lead you directly into the lives, even the thoughts and feelings, of the animals around you, the world of the plants they depend on, and the dynamics of the landscape they live in. You will find that tracking involves the nature of perception itself and will foster a stronger awareness of yourself and your own relationship with the world.

Tracking is a body of knowledge that reaches back to the roots of human consciousness and was critical to human survival. All hunter-gatherer cultures practiced animal tracking, but the Apaches of the American Southwest perhaps brought it to its highest form. As a child, I was tantalized by the few stories I read of their legendary tracking ability: finding game with the slightest signs on the landscape, reading the secrets of nature at a glance, moving invisibly on the land. If I was not in school, I was running the hills, stalking animals, pretending to be an Indian. Cochise, the famous Chiricahua chief, was one of my earliest heroes.

I knew there must be a way to enter the old world of the tracker. I searched the Boy Scout literature. I read endless animal stories. I looked for tracks on my own. But I could only find hints and second-hand information. It was a mute book of fading knowledge. Though I didn't realize it, I was witnessing the near loss of this legacy, as the last hunter-gatherer cultures were rapidly disappearing all over Earth. I didn't know how to hear the earth speak, and I gave up on it as I grew up.

Except for a few thin threads of old ways that persisted, the art of tracking in our modern world was nearly lost by the early 1900s.

One Apache scout, however, a man named Stalking Wolf, followed a vision that he was responsible for keeping these skills alive and passing them on before they were lost forever. He spent his life traveling the continent, distilling the knowledge of tracking, the skills of invisible survival, and the wisdom of Native Americans. He was truly one of the last links to native tracking and one of its greatest masters. In his eighties, Stalking Wolf found Tom Brown Jr., an eight-year-old boy growing up in the New Jersey Pine Barrens Wilderness, and selected him to receive this body of knowledge over a ten-year mentorship.

Tom went on to found a tracking and wilderness skills school and wrote a series of books that brought these skills into modern Western culture. Discovering these books in my forties, I was amazed to find exactly the information I had been looking for thirty years earlier. I quickly began practicing, with immediate and startling results. Encouraged, I began flying to the New Jersey Pine Barrens for an extensive series of Tom's classes spanning ten years, working my way from tracking basics to expert awareness and the distillation of Native American spirituality that Stalking Wolf (who Tom always respectfully refers to as Grandfather) had taught.

In those classes, Tom had a disconcerting way of loading us up with great amounts of information and sending us home thinking we were experts. I would come back from one of Tom's deep immersions full of inspiration and enthusiasm. I'd head out to the hills to apply some of what I'd learned and quickly discover that it was far more complicated than I'd imagined. I was lost. It was difficult to make progress and easy to get discouraged. In spite of my familiarity and comfort in nature, tracking involved a level of observation that was new to me. I realized that I needed to work with some local trackers.

Luckily, one of Tom's earliest students, Jon Young, had recently moved to California and started a series of tracking classes not too far away. I eagerly signed up, attending these low-key sessions with a small group who would gather from all over the state. We made a lot of progress through the power of the collective, combining our curiosity and observation. I realized that tracking is a social activity as well as a personal journey. I knew I needed to find closer kindred spirits to join in this study if I was going to continue to progress. Even in the best classes and workshops, there was not enough time to rub shoulders with experienced trackers to make sense of this complex and subtle world.

It was around then, ten years ago, that I started a local tracking club based in the Point Reyes National Seashore, an environment characterized by a Mediterranean climate with dry summers and rainy winters. I spread the word about the Marin Tracking Club, soon assembling a core group. I realized that I had tapped into a growing desire in our society to more authentically connect to nature and the earth, and that the old tracking tradition was one of the best ways to do it. There was a hunger for this information. Though trackers were few and far between out here on the West Coast, the fledgling club began growing into a community of trackers sharing this path of learning. Each month, we gathered to explore the world together.

This formed the basis of my approach to teaching, which I call "Tracking With Trackers." The key was the opportunity to debate, guess, disagree, and come to consensus with each other, each of us contributing our own experience, viewpoints, observations, and knowledge. When I started teaching, I learned far more about tracking, and about myself, than I had expected. I slowly developed my own style of instruction, of explaining my observations, connecting with others, and inspiring a passionate curiosity about our surroundings. I encourage anyone interested in tracking to find others to join them in the endeavor.

Not long after we started the tracking club, Jim Kravets, the editor of a local newspaper, the *West Marin Citizen*, asked me if I'd like to write a monthly column about nature in Point Reyes. We called it "Tracking Notes," and thus began my writing career. With Jim's help and encouragement, I got a feel for it. Eventually the column migrated to another local newspaper, the *Point Reyes Light*. It was a great opportunity to bring tracking out of the mists of the past and into modern consciousness. Through those essays, I explored the world of tracking and my relationship with it. After several years, it seemed time at last to collect and expand on those essays and gather them here.

This book is several things at once: It is a story of animals and their lives. It is a comprehensive guide to tracking and an exploration of many levels of nature awareness. It is also a journey into the spiritual skills that tracking teaches, of moving into the moment and opening the senses, of being present in everything we do, and a story of my personal journey, confronting demons and past traumas when they turn into obstacles and eventually finding the way back to my true path. This is a universal journey, and I've tried to offer some powerful tools to help anyone negotiate the trail.

My purpose has been to revive some of the tools from the old ways to bring us all closer to the earth. Tracking operates on many levels at once. It can enliven our walks in the surrounding countryside by helping us notice more of what is happening right around us. And it can bring more joy and peace into our lives as we learn how to relax and appreciate the depth and beauty of the present.

It is no small accomplishment to develop a skill that can reliably cultivate this benefit. In this simple practice lie spiritual depths that can heal our grief and troubles, and potentially our consequent physical ailments as well.

We have been raised in a culture that has largely forgotten how to heal from losses, having substituted busyness, avoidance, and material distraction for genuine health. The losses we suffer can drive us inward, into a seemingly safe but desensitized place inside our minds. This habit cuts us off from the world. Luckily, we can just jump over the back fence, or step out of the car at a trailhead, and set out on a healing journey that leads back to our own truth.

It can feel strange to drop out of our mental rush and appreciate such utterly simple and lovely things as the feel of the sun on our skin, the patterns of wind rippling through the grasses, the calls of the forest birds, and the stories in tracks, because to be present is also to take off the armor against our wounds. Taking this step creates a new depth and dimension, a relief from the flatness of our experiences when we are lost in our minds. Listening deeply into the surrounding symphony of birdcalls can elicit a profound sense of three-dimensionality in the forest, while enriching our sensitivity to the feelings and messages in individual birdcalls. Sensing the aliveness around us awakens our own aliveness. The very practice of being aware, then, is a process of becoming more alive. It cleans us up, so to speak. Nature can feel this, and tells us quickly how much it appreciates our progress by revealing more of its intimate secrets.

I invite you to immerse yourself in the stories and concepts that follow. Come back several times and read again. Move slowly, like a tracker, drink it all up, just as you will learn to do when out on the landscape.

The Tracker Mind

Tracking is a state of mind more than anything else, and there are some simple tools I use to enable my shift into a more engaged and connected relationship with nature, whether I'm alone or with a group.

These are:

1. Giving voice to gratitude and openness, and bringing our minds together.

2. Entering a state of awareness and quieted mind, moving into sensory intensification, and letting magic happen.

3. Entering the spirit of the land—envisioning the animals, how they move, where they are, and how they fit in.

4. Listening to the voice and motion of the land.

5. Observing from the three primary perspectives—flying,

standing, and kneeling.

6. Developing physical tracking skills—tracks, gaits, and pressure releases.

7. Developing sign tracking skills—scat analysis, feeding sign, digs, and runs.

8. Hitting walls and moving through them.

9. Bringing tracking into our daily lives.

These are the basic tools of animal tracking. They are well tested and reliable, and they form the outline of how I teach tracking and do tracking. These principles are woven through everything I've written in this book.

Of all the essays in this collection, this may be the most important one to read slowly, to drink up and make sure you savor and understand each point. So take your time. Relax. Let go of haste and feel yourself in each of the steps I'm about to take with you. Absorb these steps and make them your own. This will start you on a new way of enriching your experience of nature and, in the end, your experience of life.

1. First and always, I begin the shift into awareness with an intentional acknowledgment of how grateful I am to be alive and to be a part of the lovely earth and all its gifts, the greatest of which is life itself. There are many ways to make this acknowledgment, but the important thing is to do it consciously and in a spirit of cooperation and joining of minds with our companions and with all the creatures of the earth. For me, it is the start of slowing down, of opening up my senses and lighting my curiosity to see and learn new things. This is where I begin to join the interconnectedness of all things.

2. Next, I enter awareness by literally slowing myself down and walking more quietly, by slowing my breathing, and by expanding my sensory awareness. I take a moment to ground myself wherever I am, to feel the sun and wind on my skin, to listen to my surroundings,

to notice my own presence and to begin "lowering my profile," so I blend in more and become less obvious. This is how I get out of my own way and prepare to let magic happen.

3. From this place of quiet awareness, I enter the spirit of the land and begin to assess its qualities: its strengths and weaknesses in regard to different animal species, what animals are likely to live there, and where they are likely to be. I gather a sense of the recent weather patterns. I notice the shape of the land and its plant communities. I begin to envision where the animals are, how they move, and what they are doing. I start to anticipate some of what is likely to be here. I am animating this world, bringing it to life!

4. Now I begin to listen to the language and patterns of birdcalls and the whole baseline symphony of nature—both sound and motion—and tune in to the ever-changing message in it and what it can tell me. I practice walking in nature with one ear always attuned to the songs, calls, and alarms of the bird communities around me, and what their movements say about their surroundings.

5. As I move across any landscape, and begin to examine tracks, trails, and other signs of animal activity, I find it valuable to remember the three primary perspectives. First I observe the land and any particular scenario I encounter, as if I were flying over and taking in the patterns of the big picture, the Eagle's view, so I can see how the overall landscape gives meaning and context to the details I find. Then I can come in closer—but not all at once—and observe the situation from a standing viewpoint, the human viewpoint, thoroughly scanning the whole area for any relevant information. Finally it is time to come in close to the ground, the Mouse's viewpoint, and examine minute details that tell the whole story. It is easy to get too focused on the details, a state known as "focus lock," and miss obvious parts of the big picture, so I constantly shift back and forth through these different perspectives.

6. At this point, I can fully deploy my ever-growing knowledge base about the animals in the area, their habits, and how they fit into their niches. This is where I use my accumulated knowledge of each animal's foot and track morphology, its usual gait and movement pat-

terns, the tracking fundamentals such as pressure releases (the way the ground reacts to the pressure of feet in motion), track aging, and how the landscape itself dictates animal movement and the appearance of tracks. This is outright biology and physical tracking, but it is always related to my intuitive sense of the earth and my sense of where tracks are likely to be found.

7. Sign tracking requires a similar confluence of sharp, informed observation and a deep knowledge of what to expect. This is the juicy energy state that leads me into a constant parade of surprises and new revelations in nature. This is the realm of subtle feeding signs; the richness of scat content and placement; kill-site analysis; bone, feather, and fur identification; and digs, runs, and burrows. Sign tracking will often be a richer source of tracking information than actual tracks in the many areas where there is little good track substrate.

8. As I move further into the world of animal tracking, I continually confront things I don't understand and can't figure out. I can quickly reach the limits of my knowledge base and my observational skills when I'm really paying attention. It can be daunting and tiring at times, but when I start feeling exhausted or discouraged, I return to the original tools: I slow down, relax, step back a little, open my senses . . . and begin the cycle all over again. Nature is full of mystery, but I can match it with my curiosity once I learn to hold it all lightly, stay connected with my friends as well as with the earth, keep asking questions, and simply be prepared to be amazed.

9. The whole practice of tracking slows me down and reconnects me with myself. It helps me come back to my wholeness. This is a beautiful state of mind to bring back and employ in the rest of my daily life and activities, and may be the most powerful and startling benefit of tracking. It gives me a new point of view, an ability to be more patient and observe more closely than ever before. It helps me balance out the intensity, the panic, and the rush of modern human life. This gives me a higher level of mental health and clarity as well as an inner calmness that leads to greater physical health. This is full circle: this is living in gratitude.

December 2008

Before the Fall: September and October

After the long days of summer, days that seem to slow down and stretch out, the seasonal shift begins in late August. For two months, it seemed that time was suspended. But inevitably we admit that indeed the days are growing shorter, the nights are longer, and the mornings are becoming chillier.

The signs of change are subtle but abundant. The grasses, now mature, are dropping their seeds, and the lack of rain during the summer months is catching up with the landscape. The hills have turned brown. The creeks have dried up. In many parts of Point Reyes, ocean fogs provide the only source of moisture. Deciduous leaves have begun to wither. Conifers have darkened.

The coastal winds have eased from their mid-summer intensity. They are lighter now and indecisive, affording pleasant walking opportunities at any time of day. The light has been changing, too. There is a more glancing, low-angle quality to it that brings out the yellows and reds, intensifying in the foliage of shrubs and trees and in the growing mats of pine needles on the floor of the forests.

Even sound is changing. The air carries sounds differently, just as it carries the light differently. There seem to be more echoes in the air, distant sounds seem to penetrate further, birdcalls seem more plaintive and restless. The avian conversations are changing; concerns are shifting from feeding the kids to preparing for the local winter or an imminent migration, while new migratory species begin to arrive, the forefront of the major wave to come. Shorebird tracking in the esteros is exciting again: godwits, whimbrels, and curlews! The morning symphony is adding new instruments.

Most mammals have raised their kids, and they are concerned with surviving the end of the long dry season. This parched time is a hallmark of our Mediterranean climate, and, for an animal, can be as tough to endure as an East Coast winter. Food is scarce, water is scarce, and green vegetation is crowded into riparian corridors, drawing the animals that depend on these resources closer together. The animals who prey upon them have shifted correspondingly. Territorial patterns are all in great flux as the expansive cycle of the summer season slowly winds down.

Deer mice in the sand dunes display an ever-increasing hubbub of activity, harvesting seeds and caching them for winter, more and more tracks speckling the perimeters of vegetation in the morning. Vole populations in the fields have declined with the greenery. Gophers are entering a new phase of increased activity, preparing their winter runs, padding their nests, and stocking their food caches.

Bobcats and coyotes have been foraging farther in the relentless search to feed themselves and their kids. With the dry year and thinner prey populations, they have had to work a little harder, their patterns more dispersed. In just the last few days, my local family of coyotes has begun to sing with each other in the middle of the night, after a summer hiatus. Foxes have had an exceptionally successful year, perhaps benefiting from rodent populations that bulged in previous years due to big rains. Right now, they and the raccoons are busily comparing orchard maps and feasting on the fruit crops coming to maturity. Omnivore scats are full of varying seeds and skins from blackberries, huckleberries, manzanita berries, plums, and apples.

The mule deer have moved in and taken up residence, foraging through yards well into mid-day in an effort to find enough fresh vegetation to ward off starvation, teaching their young the ins and outs of the art of survival in the fall.

For my part, I feel an itch to get out and witness all of this. Nature calls me: Come hither! Change is afoot! The world is shifting! All of this—the changing angle of light, the hollow sounds, the sharp morning air, an unsettled feeling in the underbrush—takes me back to my earliest childhood memories of playing in the woods, the very air carrying the echoes of my past, haunting and brilliant. I feel my own physiology shifting, too. I want to eat and sleep more. I'm thinking about my firewood and getting things covered. Time seems more precious. I want to take it all in. Gratitude fills my heart for each living moment, for each step and breath, for each dawn. The world is alive and changing, and we are, too.

This is what I consider to be the state of grace, of living in Paradise: to be locked in with the cycle of seasonal change, feeling it in every sensory neuron. This is the state of being that is metaphorically referred to in the Genesis myth: Before the Fall, before we fell out of awareness and appreciation, before each of us became so self-conscious and lost in our minds that we no longer danced in the great cyclic rhythms, before each of us was talked into giving away our personal power. Before all of this, we walked in the Garden of Eden. Each fall, nature gives us a glimpse of the path back in.

April 2016

Going Feral

Sometimes I make a shift when I go for a walk, just after starting out. I call it "going feral." It does not take much: just a slight lean in a certain direction, a quick thought, a pause and a glance around. It can be a few steps down a trail, or a few steps out my back door. In the Tom Brown, Apache-influenced world of nature awareness, it might be called "shifting into the force." Sometimes it is called "losing your mind and coming to your senses." Whatever I call it, it is a visceral sensation that puts me into an entirely different frame of mind.

Here it is in its simplest form: get a little ways down a trail, away from the car or house. Find a spot where you can step off the trail into a little cover, maybe under the eave of some trees or behind some brush. If you have a partner who you can do this with, lucky you! Go for it. It is one of the greatest ways I know to spend time with a friend. But it is often best to be alone, because the next step is the critical one: be quiet! Quiet your chatter. Quiet your thoughts. Pay attention to where you are.

This is the shift: check into your senses; listen out around yourself; tune in; open your eyes and let the light in. Now you are shifting. Go into your primal animal self; it's always there, just under the surface, ready to awaken.

The first rule of going wild is to understand the dangers in nature and how to manage them; if you are susceptible to poison oak, make sure you know exactly what the plant looks like at any time of year. This is perhaps the first rule any animal lives by: avoid danger and injury at all costs. Have you ever noticed how cautious and careful wild animals are, how wary of anything unusual, and how reluctant they are to get in physical fights? They know well that a small injury could mean death, and they are extremely clear about the cost-to-payoff ratio involved. If you want to experience a little more wildness, take note of this. Learn to push your edges but always with a wide margin of safety and clear knowledge of the dangers involved.

So take that first step off the main path. From this spot you have chosen, just hidden from view, you can begin to shift into the mind of a deer or a coyote, aware of everything around you. Become an animal, enter your creature self. Begin to move again. Step back out onto the trail, but stay in this altered state.

Everything has changed. Feel your wildness. Every step you take sounds loud now. You instinctively walk more carefully, step more quietly, and see more clearly. You feel your kinship with all of the life forms around you: the grasses, the trees, the insects, and the birds. You also deeply feel your vulnerability and the fragility of nature under the onslaught of human power.

But we can use this human power in a reverse direction. We have great potential for providing safety to other beings. Once you begin to go feral, you touch a universal field of awareness in nature. You can project a sphere of safety that emanates from your sense of love and empathy for other lives and from your deepest sense of respect for life. Other animals will feel this, their curiosity piqued by a state so unusual for a human, and they will be drawn toward you if you can maintain it in spite of the startling close-up encounters that may occur.

Getting feral is a habit I have developed over a lifetime of being outside. Some of my earliest memories are of times, barely out of the toddler stage, when I made this shift. I felt like I had moved into the magical world of nature and felt the power of my primal animal self. I always felt welcome and safe in that world, instinctively knowing how to be quiet and slip into the wildness. I think the veil between my human self and the natural world has always been thin.

This shift can be as quick as a thought. But it does have to be intentional. It is all too easy to march out on a hike, especially with others, and continue all the talk and chatter, surely enjoying nature, but not a part of it, just a tourist. All it takes is a pause. It is a prayer to the most local god possible. It is a prayer of humility and respect, an acknowledgment of the depth and mystery of life.

Moving around like this is a dynamic meditation involving our body, mind, and spirit, all working together in what is our natural state of being human. There is a great sense of generosity, kindness, and patience in this state of mind. It is a reward in itself.

December 2016

The Bobcat

There was a bobcat trail across the sand the other day, a slow steady stride, a walking pace, laid down before dawn when the surface of the sand was wet with dew. After the day warmed up and the sand dried, the damp surface had turned into a thin crust that held its integrity late into the day. The tracks were typically feline: very round and neat without a lot of action and blowout, the result of an animal who walks carefully, using silence and stealth as its primary hunting and safety tools.

When I came upon this track, about 11 a.m., the dry surrounding sand was too loose to hold any fine detail, and the paper-thin crust would crumble at the slightest touch. But these tracks still had a crust *inside* the tracks. Each track held very exact toe and pad detail; the bobcat had pressed the damp surface sand into the walls of its tracks, where they dried in that exact shape and were protected from the degradation of midday sun and wind.

Understanding this trail and its story involved an awareness of recent weather history, knowledge of the usual bobcat rhythms in the area, and details of that specific location, forging a very accurate estimate of when the tracks were made and what the cat was doing. The slow, steady pattern indicated that she had probably already eaten her fill and was heading home along a familiar route in the heart of her established territory, without much fear or even curiosity.

A bobcat's baseline gait is a walk, steady and careful, leaving tracks in a diagonal pattern, alternating left and right. But the bobcat often walks with a slight variation: its long back legs carry its rear feet a few inches past where the front foot had stepped, an "overstep," leaving a trail of paired tracks, two right, then two left. This is the gait it uses when it is relaxed and confident. These are the things a tracker learns to read, that cause the book of nature to spring to life.

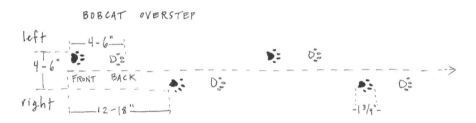

The substrate conditions that allowed me to read the bobcat prints also prove fertile for the detailed mouse tracks that remain in dry sand when there is little else to see. During their nighttime foraging journeys, the little toes and pads of the mice make precise impressions that are preserved in that fine crust when the sand dries. In downwind areas such as the Abbotts Lagoon basin, just off the Pacific Ocean, the surface sand can be so fine-grained that it can hold the imprint of a single mouse toenail. The breakdown of just a few grains of the sand can obliterate these tiny details, but the general pattern of their busy nighttime activities, the smatterings of little speckles in paths from one bush to another, can remain for days.

I have spent many hours looking at nothing but deer mouse tracks, prying open the mysteries of their activities and rhythms, even counting the tracks to determine the number of trips in their little highways. Their normal way of traveling, their baseline gait, is a bound, eight-inch-long leaps, the four feet landing in a small trapezoid shape. This is an exact miniature version of the twelve- to fifteen-foot-long bound pattern of a mountain lion in a hunting chase!

In both cases, the trapezoid shape is created in each leap, when the front feet land together and the back feet pass around and land just in front of them, resulting in a wider pair of tracks just beyond the front feet tracks. These patterns shift and change according to the conditions of the landscape and the intentions of the animal. Each species has adapted a particular, dominant style of movement, and any shift out of this baseline pattern can reveal a great deal of information about the animal at the moment it passed by. The interactions of landscape, weather, movement, and purpose create infinite variations, offering a rich document to read.

Some tracking experts, such as Louis Lieberman, who worked with native trackers in South Africa, claim that tracking and track forms inspired the beginning of written language, as primitive humans began to communicate symbolically about the animals around them. The tracks themselves may have been the original forms or models for written words and letters.

Tom Brown once showed me an ancient deer skin, at least five hundred years old, that his mentor had passed on to him, with symbols written on it by the old Apaches. It was a sort of shorthand, pictographic language conveying detailed information about deer and other animals, information that was vital to keeping people fed and safe.

Looking at the stars tonight, I can imagine proto-humans looking at this night sky a couple million years ago, their developing minds beginning to organize the starry patterns into identifiable and nameable constellations. Pattern recognition is a critical and primal part of how the human mind works, an essential tool to organize the infinite amount of information our senses gather and provide a way to communicate about it. Tracking may be nearly as old as the human brain, an essential part of our hard-wired survival skill set. When I am tracking, I can feel these ancient roots connecting me to something that is far deeper than modern concepts of living and culture.

The patience and inner stillness required to tease answers out of the constant mysteries in nature is something I bring home and remember to use in everyday life. Tracking has taught me to keep observing instead of seeking immediate answers when I confront a mystery. It has taught me to stop, stand back, and take a deep breath the moment I begin to feel confused, rushed, or pressured—and then continue asking questions! This is how nature immersion, and animal tracking in particular, can actually become a spiritual path. Nature can be our greatest teacher if we only let it. The lessons it teaches are the oldest lessons, tens of thousands of years older than modern religious concepts. As such they can be the healthiest lessons, too. This is where the beauty and magic of tracking reside. Without fail, shifting into this way of moving through nature (and our own world) will elicit new experiences and insights, giving a glimpse into the intricate interwoven life hidden just under that surface crust.

Each time I track an animal, I become that animal for a short while. I can feel how it feels, how it moves and responds, how it fits into the world. I can view life through its eyes for a moment and step on the ground through its feet. This builds a deep sense of brotherhood and familiarity, a bond that is not easily broken.

That bobcat has become a true friend, elusive for sure, seldom seen, but someone who I deeply respect. She teaches me to walk lightly upon the earth.

October 2007

The Edges

Edges are the best places to look for signs, tracks, and the richness
of life. Where the eaves of the oak trees hang over the edges of the
grassy meadow, where land meets water along the edges of a pond or
a creek, on the grassy sides of trails, along ditches and fence lines, at
the dusty sides of dirt roads, on borderlines and ridge lines, necklines
and pinch-points, wherever forest gives way to chaparral, where slope
gives way to basin. These are the places to look. These are the places
of greatest abundance and diversity. This is where the dew lingers the
longest, where the spirit resides, where both safety and adventure is
right at hand . . . and where we are most likely to find good tracks.

Our personal edges are just the same, our root-tips and leaf buds,
where we are growing and blossoming, where the richness of our
experience meets the new and unknown. Tracks are simply where
our edges contact the world around us and leave their impressions.
Every being takes up space and fits into the world in ways that have

evolved and developed for, literally, billions of years. We are all the descendants of those countless experiments with what works. Our lives are an ancient dance, genetic instructions worked out over great expanses of time, everything in nature moving like clockwork, yet in a constant state of change and adaptation.

One toe of a coyote, for example, reveals the endless plasticity of natural evolution in living forms. The size and shape of the toe and foot is a perfect balance between myriad possibilities of weight, traction, support, movement, stealth, speed, substrate, and purpose. The amazingly durable and renewable skin of a toe is designed for a lifetime of contact with the ground.

Our feet are in a constant act of rebalancing. In their edges, where they contact the earth, they reflect every nuance of motion, thought, and intention. Every part of an animal is intimately tied to the earth. The landscape has created each living being, fitting it into the jigsaw puzzle of inter-related life, and its tracks can reveal the whole story of that animal—where it is, what it is doing, why it belongs to that particular location, how it moves, how it lives.

Here is a simple and revealing experiment that we tried at one of Tom Brown's classes. Don't just think about this; actually get up and do it! Right now! Do it a few times and let it sink in.

Try this—really! Take your socks off and go stand on a cold floor. Feel your feet in contact with the floor. Tune into them. Now, lift your left arm. Whoosh! You can feel a wave of pressure across the soles of your feet as your body reflects and rebalances every part of that movement. Do it again! As your left arm moves out, you can feel your weight shift over to the right side of your feet. The contrast of a cold floor with your warm feet accentuates the sensations.

Now just turn your head. Feel the ripple again? Now just gulp! Even that can be felt in your feet, a wave of adjustment that sweeps down through your legs and feet and into the ground, where it is expressed in our tracks. If you add in motion, intentions, thoughts, feelings, and reactions, you realize that at your edges, in your tracks, there is a complete record of who you are and what you are doing. With practice, careful observation, and good substrate, tracks reveal the whole range of living action in plates and fissures around the edges of the track, in waves and discs in the toe and heel pads, and minor shudders and ridges in the floor of the track. These are called "pressure releases," and they are what bring a track to life.

It is one thing to look at drawings of tracks in a book, and another thing entirely to read real tracks that living animals created, on variable substrates in complex environments. It immediately tests our perceptual limits. If we take the time to walk out to these edges and spend time with them, we will discover something within ourselves as well—a source of endless new growth and aliveness.

There are few perfect tracks in nature. They are beautiful to see when you find them, but we usually find only partial tracks, barely visible tracks, minute distortions in the soil or small bends in the leafy debris on a forest floor. The light can be tricky, making a track invisible in anything but the perfect angle. The ground might be rough, dry, covered with debris, or too loose to hold any detail. It is easy to get lost out at these edges. But this is also where we are most alive, where we are increasing our knowledge, growing our wisdom, expanding our limits, sending out new roots and shoots.

A good tracker cannot afford to be an expert. To indulge in claims of superior knowledge is to retreat from these learning edges into complacency, and that is precisely when nature, in her most coyote trickster fashion, will fool us badly and throw us off the trail. The essence of a good tracker is humility, gratitude, and an open mind. There is no need to be an expert—it only gets in the way and distracts from the beautiful miracles right in front of us. Out at our edges, where we are learning to be alive and to open up and connect with the earth, we have a chance to break away from the compulsion to live in our minds, to separate and divide. Tracking provides an avenue for living in a connected way, entirely in the present, no props or equipment required. It opens the door to our own primal roots.

Pushing these edges can be exhausting, difficult, scary, and . . . extremely joyful. It is liberating to free yourself from the burden of knowing, to instead become a constant student, open to all the lessons the earth has to teach. It is essentially the same as falling in love. The heart opens and gives itself to something entirely new and different. The voice of the earth speaks. There is no fear in vulnerability, because nature contains the ultimate safety and assurance for opening your heart; it is like coming home to a place we have always known, a return to paradise. This is where tracking and love come together. In this place, it is possible to see someone's inner spirit, their true essence, to love them simply for who they are, and equally, to find the same love for oneself. One feeds the other. It is impossible to love the earth and hate oneself. It is impossible to love oneself and hate the earth. And it is impossible to go tracking without falling in love.

July 2010

After the Fall: The First Awakening—
November and December

The hills are aglow! The clock is reset. The shift is on. After the long, drawn-out rainless season that stretched from late spring to a dead-dry autumn, the early rains finally arrived and transformed the world. I call this the First Awakening.

With unusual suddenness, the hills and fields have burst forth with new grasses, forbs, flowers, rhizomes, roots, and runners. Everywhere you look, the plants have awakened. Look at the slopes and fields; on a sunny day, the grasses shine with an almost neon vibration. Their biological clockworks set in motion, seeds are sprouting, and roots and shoots are growing fast, taking advantage of the fine line between increasing moisture and decreasing light.

The intense photosynthesis fueling their rush to take advantage of precious dwindling light has re-colored the landscape from the yellow-brown of spent grasses to rolling carpets of glowing green sprouts.

Coyote brush has flowered, now covered in succulent new growth. Lupine remembers that spring will come again and begins putting out tender new leaves. Wild strawberry sends out new mats of runners.

Immediately, all the animals—mammals, reptiles, birds, and insects, lives entwined in botanical rhythms—burst into a flurry of action themselves. In the new grasses, voles, gophers, and rabbits are already giving birth to new litters, re-establishing runs, and making new burrows. Insects burst forth too, laying eggs, hatching larvae of infinite variation, and growing fat and nutritious with the abundance of the rains. Hawks and owls sweeping down the southward migration routes are taking advantage of the rodent boom. Local raptors know there is plenty to share. Ravens and crows, along with skunks, opossums, and foxes, are feasting on the new forage. Gophers, frogs, and coyote youth are setting off on long dispersal journeys.

Meanwhile, another cycle is set into motion—courting season begins. Less daunted by the wet and cold of coming winter than the hunger in the dry season, many animals are suddenly waking up to the urge to procreate. Coyotes and foxes begin running in close pairs, stride for stride, gathering with friends in outdoor nightclubs on hilltops and in basins. I can see the big smiles, the tongues hanging out.

The bobcats, as you'd expect, are more subtle. The big males cruise a little more deeply into female territories, starting the timeless process of selection and stimulation that initiates reproduction. Where substrate is favorable, it is a great prize to find the tracks of courting pairs, larger tracks dancing alongside smaller tracks.

Deer, of course, have matured and moved through the rutting season. By now, a lot of pairs have already mated, while some are still trying, the very trying necessary to stimulate and complete all the hormonal processes. The exhausting rut depletes the energy stored up in the fall, and the bucks are glad for the new abundance to start the process of rebuilding their strength. The does are building up their reserves for the long haul of birthing and child-rearing to come soon enough in the spring.

It is a grand time of year, the ancient and intricate jigsaw puzzle of life on earth never so apparent as after the fall, after the sweet, quiet— and deadly—time just two months ago. It is a strange time of the year, so intense and quick, like the front edge of a squall tearing across the land. The world wakes up from a drowsy slumber and springs into action, like someone late for work, to make the most of this precious window before the trough of winter brings pause again.

When we really grasp the beauty and complexity of these shifting gears, the shorter days and howling storms are not so bothersome. Instead, they become a further source of magic and intrigue, of awe and appreciation. What an amazing thing to witness: the reawakening of the earth!

There is no shame in this fall, no expulsion from Eden, no fall from Grace. Rather the opposite. It is a fall into grace. The earth welcomes us home like no heaven ever will. If you think about it for a moment, you will remember that each of us is literally a descendant of a free-living hunter-gatherer. Despite the inherent struggles of survival, at one time we all regarded the earth and the balance of its living systems as sacred and felt that we were responsible for its welfare. We all belong to the earth. We arose from this earth along with all other life forms.

Since the dawn of human consciousness, we wondered why we were here and how we fit in. We wondered where we came from and where we went. Every group had its creation story. But as human social structures became more complex and required more centralized planning, civilizations drifted into a tragic misconception about the earth in order to defend the violence and conquest (both social and environmental) inherent in agriculture and stratified social classes. They had to justify social inequity and the toilsome life by distorting our intrinsic relationship with the Earth and institutionalizing that distortion in religious concepts that required a feeling that we did not belong here, that the Earth is nothing more than a resource for us to exploit and discard on our way to something else.

To maintain this illusion and legitimize extreme wealth disparity, modern societies created a parallel spiritual hierarchy that gave hope for salvation in life after death—a misconception we live with to this day. In the end, we are supposed to believe that "God" banished his own creation—us—from the paradise he had created for us, for sins he had to have known we would commit. The story makes no sense because it puts forth an insane premise—that we were born flawed and have to atone for this by suffering in a land we were not meant to be a part of.

Poppycock! Look outside. This is heaven and each of us is a part of it! This time of shifting seasons and quickening life cycles makes it ever more apparent and available. Make of it what you will. It is up to you. Take a walk. Slow down. Open your eyes and ears. Listen to the birds! Embrace the world and make it your own. Breathe and be glad! Realize that the self-criticisms you carry around are simply burdens you were given without your consent, by mentors who didn't know what they were doing, who passed on the same unexamined falsehoods they were taught. Once you decide to believe in yourself for a moment, you will see what I mean. The wonderment of a living earth that you belong to is right at hand, perhaps more now than any other season of the year.

February 2016

Coyotes

The dunes at Abbotts Lagoon are like one of those old Disney nature movies, where the stroke of a brush across the canvas paints an entire landscape. The weather and seasons become the brush, painting animal tracks that shift in ever-changing progression. One month it's all mice and bobcats. Another month it's all skunks and opossums.

It was all coyote last time, early on a chilly January morning. Damp sand showed great track detail. Other tracks were virtually absent, but the coyotes were dancing all over the dunes, playing with each other in wild abandon. Their tracks—crisscrossing the clean, rain-washed expanse in single trails, beautiful duets, and small groups—showed outright playfulness: pouncing, running, and rapid gait changes, from walk to trot to lope and back to a walk in the space of a few yards. They were literally kicking up their heels, the sand sprayed out in all directions around their tracks. They would sometimes circle around together and sit down, as if to admire their handiwork, leaving beautiful sit prints. It was like a textbook on how coyotes move.

Coyote courtship season begins in early winter here, and that night it was in full swing. Three days later, the coyotes and their tracks were gone, and the smaller animals began to emerge again, leaving tentative scatterings of tracks, close to cover.

Coyotes use many different gaits, revealing the range of their moods, thoughts, and intentions, and their movements can be used as a foundation for studying animal gaits in general. The normal, or baseline, gait of a coyote is a trot. It trots through its territory for hours at a time, following scents on the wind, moving from one hunting area to another, gobbling up great distances, while keeping an eye out for the sudden movement of a rabbit bolting. One of its traveling gaits, peculiar to canines, is called a "side trot," where it angles its hind end out to one side, so its back feet can more easily pass by the front feet as it trots. This leaves a very characteristic track pattern, where the footprints of the front feet are all on one side of the line of travel and the rear prints are on the other side.

COYOTE SIDETROT

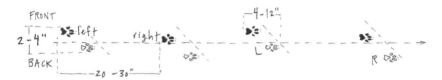

Just as you will find yourself shifting and adjusting your backpack as you hike along a trail, the coyote will shift back and forth from left side to right side, to a center trot and back again. In one quick balletic movement, it will shift sides, one or two slightly more tiptoed tracks being the only indication of the actual weight shift.

As you think about these things, you may notice yourself changing your gait as your mood or plan changes. Think about how you move when you're in a hurry to make it to the grocery store before it closes. Then watch the difference in your stride when you leave a restaurant after a good meal.

Coyote gaits have also adapted to its prey. I flushed a jackrabbit out of its snug little shelter under a low coyote bush in the lee of the wind one evening recently, watching in admiration at how it escaped, its explosive, dodging bounds mixed with startling bursts of speed. The coyote, co-evolving with the rabbits for eons, has developed an ability to run in variable gaits that mimic the rabbit's evasive tactics, with the ability to twist, turn, and rapidly accelerate.

When a coyote slows down to a walk, it is often because it wants to check out a scent or inspect some signs of prey. The coyote slow walk or stalk usually shows an "overstep" pattern, where the hind foot is placed well ahead of where the front foot has just stepped. For the coyote, the gangly-legged runner, the overstep walk indicates that it is focusing on something, moving unusually slowly.

This is in beautiful contrast to the bobcat, who crosses the dunes frequently to hunt around the edges of the lagoon. Her baseline gait is a walk. She is a stealth hunter. She stops and listens often. She stays behind cover, where she remains hidden even in daylight. Her normal traveling gait is an overstep.

You can follow her tracks and see the overstep pattern expand when she hurries. Perhaps it was late, and she was a little worried about crossing an open area, or maybe she heard some coyotes in the distance. When she relaxes and slows down again, the overstep shrinks. When she really slows down, approaching a hunting area or intently listening to the surroundings, she drops into a "direct register" walk, where the back foot steps precisely, and silently, into the track the front foot just made.

Sometimes, when she wants to speed up and cross an exposed area, she breaks into an undulating lope. I think we've all seen this at night when a neighborhood cat dashes across a road as we drive up. She starts out in a choppy little fast walk, looking like she has six or eight legs. Then halfway across the street, her speed has increased to the point where she shifts into that lope, which carries her to the safety of cover on the other side of the road.

The coyote, on the other hand, is not as secretive as the bobcat and regularly crosses open ground in his beautiful arcs, following the contours of the landscape and the scents on the wind, almost as if flying low over the land like a northern harrier. In trails like this, you can truly see the land directing the animal. Clearly, he has little fear of being seen and caught, so confident is he in his speed and his ability to cover great distances.

But as the seasons shift, the patterns change again as the coyotes move into their denning and birthing cycles. Their trails are less exuberant and more secretive. We may begin to find the youthful tracks of the kids tagging along as the season progresses. I find great comfort in these ancient patterns. The very thought of those old webs of interrelatedness, playing themselves out in timeless progression, relaxes my heart and lets me breathe more deeply.

January 2008

Gaits and Movement

Animal gaits and gait patterns are a critical part of tracking. They help us understand who made a trail and what they were doing. It is one of the critical keys to bringing the stories in nature to life. When you understand how an animal moves to make a certain track pattern and grasp the mechanics of movement, that animal will appear like a holograph right before your eyes. The relationship between gait patterns and the pressure releases the animal creates in its contact with the earth offers a highly accurate interpretation of its movements and purposes.

Native cultures all over the earth placed high value on understanding how animals moved. They practiced moving like the animals they hunted because it helped them understand the animal itself and the meaning of its tracks. As modern trackers, we can learn how these gaits work by doing them ourselves. Gaits can express emotions: a trot is often a sign of a more purposeful feeling, while a lope, though higher intensity, can reflect a more relaxed state of mind.

Gaits are simply different ways of moving. They are related to speed, but there is wide overlap between gaits and speeds. Animal gaits range by speed from a walk to a trot and out into a lope, a gallop and a bound, much like the gears of a bike. There are dozens of variations on these basic gaits, and most animals will use several of them in the course of their daily activities. A mouse will use a walk, a trot, a lope, and a bound. A coyote will trot for great distances but shift into a very slow walk when carefully hunting. Yet it is important to understand that each animal has a baseline gait—its most habitual way of traveling, the kind of movement that works best according to its place in the tapestry of nature.

Each of these gaits has precise, predictable mechanical patterns that are similar whether used by a mouse or a mountain lion. That can be hard to believe when you see a mouse scurry across your floor in a startling burst of speed or watch a dog trotting, because their feet are just a blur. But in a clean substrate, like sand, the story can be seen. Each foot lands in a clear repetitive pattern. Assessing a gait pattern with a consideration of dimensions, location, terrain, and context can yield a very accurate identification of the animal and an assessment of its purposes and state of mind, without the need for clear track detail.

Let's start with the basics: yourself. As two-legged primate, your natural gait, your baseline, is . . . a walk. One, two, one, two . . . right, left, right, left. The most basic gait. But your speed can vary widely. You can move anywhere between a very slow and a very fast walk. The slowest end of a walk would be a careful stalk, perhaps even tiptoeing. This can be extremely slow, approaching a virtual standstill, but a walking gait nevertheless: one foot after another, one step at a time.

Speeding up to a normal walk, such as walking down a trail or a sidewalk, you hit an easy stride and pace. You are loosely swinging along. This is baseline. Each foot makes its stride, stepping, leaving the ground, swinging forward and landing again, before the other foot leaves the ground. There is always one foot on the ground. This defines a walk.

HUMAN WALK

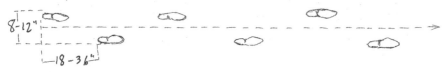

8-12"

18-36"

Now you need to hurry: you see that you are running a little late. You speed up the walk, same rhythm, just faster. You are beginning to see that you might not make it through the door before it closes. You speed up to maximum walk speed: one, two, one, two, one, two…

At a certain point, you just have to shift into the next gear: a trot. It's the same rhythm—one, two, one, two—but there is a critical difference. Now, you are pushing off a little harder and making a small leap with each step. Both feet are in the air for a moment before your landing foot hits the ground. You are airborne between steps. Also, notice that though you are moving faster than you were in your fast walk, your strides are slower!

As you swing along in this new pace, you begin to warm up and hit an easy natural stride, the baseline trot, the pace that, if you are fit, as any healthy wild animal is, will carry you for miles. Intent is always a part of a gait. The purpose of a trot is to cover some distance and get somewhere, whereas the walk has a wider range of purposes, from simply looking around to having a destination to reach.

FAST TROT - HUMAN

4-6"

36-54"

Speed that trot up and you enter the human run. In our case it is still just a one, two, one, two rhythm, but at a higher quantum level, a higher energy output, with obviously longer stride lengths. If you look at the pressure releases, you can see the higher level of pent-up energy in each landing and push-off, more energy expended with each step. The other characteristic of gaits and speed is that the straddle—the width of the trail, the distance between left and right—narrows with increasing speed. This is nearly universal in animal movement.

Now, let's take this over to the world of the four-legged. There is another dimension here, but the walk and trot are much the same, only with an extra set of legs, as if someone were walking right behind you, stride for stride. It starts with a walk, called a direct-register walk, where the back feet land right in, or very close, to the track the front foot just made. The pattern is called a diagonal walk (or trot) because the tracks are diagonal to each other. One foot moves at a time, so it is a 1,2,3,4; 1,2,3,4; 1,2,3,4 rhythm. It is very stable because at any one moment, three feet are on the ground forming a tripod, and only one is moving, except for an instantaneous moment when a front foot lifts and is replaced by a back foot.

The tracks are diagonal from each other, alternating right and left. But once the animal speeds up a little, it makes a natural shift into a trot. The tracks still have a diagonal pattern but now the animal is in a different rhythm: 1,2,1,2,1,2. Now the feet are landing two at a time, front right and rear left in one beat, front left and rear right on the next beat. The body movement has a choppy look. There is a very particular choreography that has to take place so the feet move smoothly without getting tangled up.

Raccoons are a unique exception. With their emphasis on using their hands to explore for food, they have a style of walking that places greater weight on their back feet, and this has produced a gait in which they move both feet on one side, before moving the feet on the other side, called a 2x2 walk or trot. This results in a track pattern of paired tracks, with a rear track alongside a front track, alternating left and right.

2 x 2 WALK — RACCOON

The next gear up in speed and intensity is the lope. This is the familiar undulating, "rocking horse" movement, a graceful gait, relaxed in appearance, with the head bobbing up and down with each stride and tracks that separate out into four-track groups.

There are several variations of the lope, and each animal has its preferred, most common style. I love the names of them. There are: two-by-two lopes, three-by-four lopes, transverse lopes, and rotary lopes. But in all cases, the lope is a continuous series of little leaps: the animal (whether skunk or coyote) pushes off its back feet and leaps forward in a stretch, front feet reaching out and all four feet in the air for a moment. It lands on the front feet, and the back feet come forward around the front feet, bunching the body, to land again and start another leap. The feet land in a new undulating rhythm: 1234—1234—1234.

The familiar rippling movement of a skunk crossing a field comes from its loping gait, tail waving as the head bobs up and down, reflecting their lack of fear or concern. Coyotes will often use this gait too, fast but unhurried and unafraid.

As an animal speeds up even more, it gradually shifts into a gallop. The sequence of steps in the tracks of a lope is front/back/front/back. As the speed increases, the rear feet land farther and farther ahead until both rear feet are landing ahead of both front feet with each stride. Now the sequence is front/front/back/back. This is the definition of a gallop—it is simply a high-speed lope, with the same stretch-and-gather rhythm.

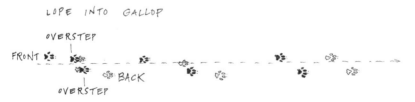

The final gait to consider is the bound, which is really just a high-energy version of a lope. In the bound, the front feet land to-gether and the back feet come around them on the outsides and also land together. Since both feet are leaping and pushing off together, it is the most powerful gait and commonly used for fast acceleration, such as when a bobcat charges after prey from a crouch or is startled and makes a fast getaway. It is an explosive gait and usually will have great scatterings of soil around the tracks. Dogs commonly start out with a bound to accelerate when chasing a stick.

BOUND VARIATIONS

In fact, playing fetch with a dog will reveal a complete cycle of gaits: the initial high-acceleration bound, shifting to a big lope once the speed is attained, a pounce on the stick, and a high-headed trium-phant trot back to its owner, slowing to a walk for the final approach to drop the stick. Try it on a beach a few times and track it out careful-ly—it is a complete lesson!

April 2009

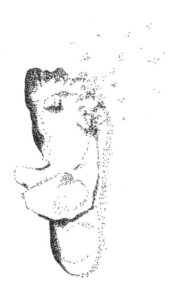

The Theory of Pressure Releases

One of the most elegant aspects of tracking is the art of reading the living movements of an animal in how the ground responds to the pressure of its steps. This is how the ground speaks. This art, brought to its highest level by the Apaches in the Southwest, was nearly lost with the rapid decline of native culture in the face of advancing Europeans. Luckily Stalking Wolf, the Apache scout, had the life vision of distilling this knowledge and passing it on.

Hunter-gatherers all over the earth, including the local Ohlone and Coast Miwok, had an intimate sense of connection with the natural world. All of them had highly developed skills in tracking and awareness, but the Apache stand out for the depths and complexities to which they took the art of tracking. We are very fortunate to have access to this legacy.

It is deeply satisfying to learn to recognize the tracks, signs, and patterns of the animals all around us, in ways that our predecessors did. It brings a fundamental sense of re-orientation, providing a compass that points to an inner true north, no matter how topsy-turvy our world may seem to be.

There is great personal value in learning to see the interconnections in nature—how the wind affects the birds, how the birds affect the mammals, how the course of each season affects the plants and in turn affects the insects, birds, mammals, ourselves. This is the real world, a home to come back to.

But beneath track identification and gait analysis, there is something going on inside of every track, a set of universal principles defining how the earth reacts to motion and shifting weight. These principles, the "pressure releases," are the same whether the substrate is wet or dry, hard or soft, clean or covered with debris. They are the same whether we are barefoot or wearing shoes! Pressure releases are the result of legs and feet interacting with the earth to create movement.

Movement is astoundingly complex. In the course of any one stride, multiple thoughts and feelings are shifting and changing, whether it is you or I, a deer, a bobcat, a bird, or a beetle. Dozens of muscles in our feet and legs are contracting and relaxing with each step, creating the dynamic process of balance and movement.

With patient study, we can learn how the earth records this process and how to read it. The Apaches perfected this art over hundreds of generations. In the open landscapes of the desert Southwest, they were able to carefully observe moving animals and correlate those movements to the details in the resulting tracks. Since tracking animals was so fundamental to survival in those environments, they developed a complex understanding of motion and its expression in tracks. This visual language can be learned by slowly building up a vocabulary that enables us to see and understand tracks. This is when the tracks begin to tell their story.

From the time a foot lands during a step until it leaves the ground again, every head turn, arm swing, hesitation, change of plan, or shift of balance is recorded in the ground. The actual track we see is the last moment of the step, when the foot finally pushed off and left the ground, but all of the other aspects of the step, from first contact with the ground through the whole motion of the stride, leave deformities in the ground that can be read as well.

The subtleties of intention, the context of the situation, and the actual substrate on which a track is made are infinitely complex; it can seem mind-boggling to interpret. There is no solution other than committed observation and experience, as well as a clear understanding of the principles involved. Slowly it starts to make sense, and eventually you will learn to dive deeply into the story of the tracks at your first glance.

For a start, find some clean damp ground, damp sand at a beach perhaps, that will record very clear tracks. Or build a tracking box at home, an eight-foot-long box of two-by-sixes that you can fill with clean sand. Take a few steps across this ground. Start, walk slowly, speed up, stop. Simplify this until you can go back and look at specific steps, remembering what you did.

You will quickly notice that when you walk forward, a disc-shaped section of soil (or sand) is pushed back in the direction of your heel, just behind your toes. The faster you walk, the longer this disc is, until it can be as long as the whole track at a fast walk or trot. The size of the disc, relative to the qualities of the substrate, is an incredibly precise indicator of speed and acceleration. It cannot be otherwise. The ground is recording everything. Our challenge is to learn how to read it.

Now try a couple of sharp turns. You will notice a plate of soil pushed off to the side of the track, caused by the sideways pressure of the foot against the ground. This plate can be any size, from almost invisibly minute, a few grains of dust, to huge and obvious, larger than the track itself, depending on the force of the turn and the nature of the ground.

These two pressure releases, the disc and the plate, are where the tracks begin to come to life and the earth begins to speak. Once you begin to see this, the ground will never look the same again. Now, when you look at the tracks of a coyote who crossed a landscape, you will begin to see the discs and plates, as well as fissures and crumbles, that tell the story of its thoughts, feelings, and reactions, revealing its intentions and predicting where it will head next. You've begun a journey that can carry you far.

When you follow a deer trail, you will see that the hoof edges, and the inner soft pads as well, have left similar distortions in and around the tracks. But they will have a completely different personality than your own tracks because of how differently a deer moves and how different its purposes and concerns are. This is the level where all the details inform us, and the whole picture comes together to tell the story of this particular animal. The pressure releases make sense in terms of the animal who made the tracks, the time and place it made them, and the gaits it was using. All of these details begin to sing the same tune, so to speak, when we listen carefully. Just as the track and its major pressure releases have to fit together, the minor pressure releases must agree too. We are looking at a holistic life played out in the motions of the animal, so details that don't fit the story may be telling us we don't yet have the right interpretation. When everything adds up, when you hear that harmonious tune, and it plays from one track to another, you know you are indeed on the right track.

January 2011

The Language of Pressure Releases

Now let's go outside and look at animal tracks. Find some tracks and follow them. Make more of your own tracks. Compare your own tracks to wild animal tracks every chance you get. Persist in studying your own tracks over and over, until you are very familiar with how they reflect your own movements. Then work on comparisons with other animals. You'll begin to relate your own movement with all animal movement and see the universal principles expressed in the reaction of ground to foot pressure.

It can quickly become complicated and overwhelming, so always simplify if you begin to feel discouraged! Study simple, straight-line walking until you can quickly and easily recognize the effects of slowing down and speeding up, starting and stopping, and maintaining various speeds. Take time with each test. Observe. Let it sink in. Let your mind begin to grasp it. It may take years.

Your greatest ally in this, as in all tracking, is your unconscious awareness. Your mind is registering far more sensory information, and possibly intangible sensations, than you will ever consciously notice. But your unconscious mind is not inaccessible. It is simply another aspect of your own knowledge and awareness. We must remember this. Unconscious awareness is our friend and will do much of our work for us, but we have to allow it. This is what slowing down and "shifting into the force" is all about: opening an ongoing dialogue with our other levels of awareness and letting them speak. The unconscious mind is where you will notice patterns, connect layers of information, and remember past observations that help interpret the present story.

The principles of movement are always the same, but all surfaces are different and react differently. Ground is rarely flat. Hardness and dryness of ground can vary dramatically from one step to another. Tracks begin to weather, from the moment they are made, at varying rates. Movement is infinitely dynamic. Animals are not robots. Every second is a moment of life and spontaneous creation. A world of change occurs from the beginning to the end of every step and the ground is recording it.

We have to simplify, take it one piece at a time, and begin to sort it out. Our brain is designed precisely for such a task, having evolved out of this very need to make sense of the world. In the pressure releases, we are simply advancing the art of awareness.

Pressure releases reflect three general types of movement:

1. Major movement includes starting, stopping, acceleration and deceleration, speed, direction changes and head position, which all create primary pressure releases.

2. Transition movement includes anticipation, gait changes, and mid-stride adjustments, such as re-balancing or other secondary efforts during a stride, which create secondary pressure releases (or even third or fourth level pressure releases) in the toes and heels of the tracks, as well as secondary plates around the edges.

3. Micro movements involve thoughts and feelings, hesitations and reactions, as well as the internal health and the

age of an animal. These all create sub-pressure releases expressed as shudders, ridges, tiny valleys, and pocks in the floor of the tracks. Sometimes these can be extremely small and hard to see, but they can also be quite obvious.

Major Movement: Discs, Dishes, Plates, and Slopes

Take a few steps forward and stop. The essential elements of a track and its pressure releases are already here. There is the floor of the track, the sidewalls, and the overall track at ground level. When a foot presses into the ground, some of the ground surface is compressed downward and some is pressed outward.

The foot lands, rolls, and then pushes off. The foot is in a constant process of rebalancing weight shifts that the body is experiencing. The pressure releases are the effects of that rebalancing: the greater the force, the greater the effects.

1. The Disc

During a step, the foot creates a wave in the floor of the track. As the foot pushes off, the toes and ball of the foot push against the wave and break off a round disc of soil in the front of the track. As speed increases up to a fast walk, the rear edge of the disc goes through several levels of greater distortion from fissuring to crumbling and finally to exploding at a jog pace.

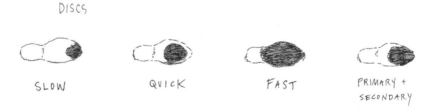

DISCS

SLOW   QUICK   FAST   PRIMARY +
                                            SECONDARY

2. The Dish

Pick up the pace some more and another level of pressure release occurs. The whole front of the floor of the track shears off and pushes backward in the track, creating a "dish" that can spread into the back of the track and goes through increasing levels of intensity with fissures, crumbling, and explosions. Deceleration and stopping create backward discs within the track and plates out to the front.

After you feel comfortable with the basics of starting and walking, you can consider acceleration. Take it slowly again. Start at a slow walk and then accelerate to a fast walk. It only takes a few steps. In the actual strides that increase speed, the increased pressure will create significantly larger discs and dishes in the track. Once the new speed is attained, the discs shrink back to what is appropriate only to maintain the new speed. It is critical to understand that the pressure releases express the amount of force put into each step, and thus the acceleration force creates larger distortions.

Very importantly, the strides will lengthen during the acceleration and hold the new length at the new speed, and the discs will be larger at higher speeds due to the greater amount of force required to maintain the higher speed and longer strides.

This is where we collide with the real world. Uphill movement creates discs that are much the same as those created by acceleration, and they are highly variable depending on substrate conditions. When we apply this to wild animals, their tracks are very likely to be going uphill or downhill, often in rapid sequence as the topography varies, so you always must factor in this aspect.

Deceleration and stopping are much the reverse of speed increase and maintenance, with corresponding reverse discs. Once acceleration is understood and recognizable, slowing and stopping will make sense. Slowing puts pressure against the front edge of the track, so here we begin to move into the world of plates, the reaction of soil outside of the track outline. But let's look at one more aspect of forward motion before we launch into plates.

3. The Slope

The last aspect of forward motion and track floor has to do with the way that feet compensate for changes in position of the head. Head up and down are easy to grasp: when the head points down, the floor of the track tilts forward. More pressure is put on the toes and the front end of the foot. When the head looks up, the floor of the track slopes backward.

SLOPE

TOES DOWN

Try this yourself and look. Do it over and over until you see the common elements. Then notice the floor tilt in wild tracks. You will notice this tilt often with coyote tracks; the floor of the tracks will tilt forward as they trot along with their nose close to the ground, but it will shift farther back when they lift their head to look around.

A similar but more complicated element in reading a track is the effect of sideways movement of the head or arms. When the head of a coyote shifts to the side, it is the same as if we raise our arm out to the side. At first, the feet press down on that side to hold up the new weight, but then the body has to tilt in the opposite direction to counterbalance the weight shift, and the track flattens out again.

When you try this with your own tracks, simply stand loosely and slowly raise your right arm. Step away and examine your tracks. You see not only the tilted floor of your tracks but the dynamics of the weight shift itself. Again, don't complicate it too much at first. Take it one step (literally) at a time. But soon you will be able to look around as you walk, then go back and see which steps reflect that dynamic motion. The tilt of the floor will indicate where an animal was looking. This will be corroborated by the trail itself and the landscape around it.

4. The Plate

Now we are going to move outside of the track outline. This is a big move, bringing in an extremely important pressure release that provides much more definition to movement. Take a couple of steps in a good clean substrate and make a 45-degree turn to the right.

Check this out. Do it over and over. Simply observe the effects of one direction shift. Around the heel and the toe, the turning force causes a disc of soil to fracture and slide out over the ground surface around the edge of the track: a plate.

Depending on the speed and intensity of the turn, as well as the quality of the substrate, this plate can be anywhere from a slight ridge along the edge of the track to a plate that is larger than the track itself. The intensity is also expressed in the fissures, cracks, and crumbles on the outer edge of the plate. The extreme expression of intensity is the "explosion," when very violent and sudden changes in momentum occur. It can be in a sudden explosive start, a sudden stop, or a quick change in direction. The plates that result are blown out and scattered.

These plates, being outside of the track border, are often useful in determining which of two trails was laid down first. There will often be one track that threw a direction or weight-shift plate, which crosses over a previously made track, making it clear that it came afterwards.

PLATES

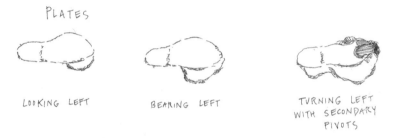

LOOKING LEFT   BEARING LEFT   TURNING LEFT
                                            WITH SECONDARY
                                                PIVOTS

Transition Movement: Secondary Pressure Releases

Now we are going to move a little deeper into the track itself. Feet, even when in shoes, are very dynamic, and all parts of a foot are involved in movement. Just as the whole track expresses all of the subtleties of changing motion, the inner parts of the foot do too. The toes and heel of a foot will reflect change of direction, change of speed and gait, and reactions to the world around that moment.

These are not hard to see if you look. Again—best barefooted now—make a few turns in clean damp sand. Don't over-complicate it. Now look carefully at the details in and around each toe, around the ball of the foot and the heel. A classic and easy-to-see pressure release is a sideways wave in the ridge between toes, where the toes pushed sideways to power the turn. Again, do it over and over until it becomes familiar and then go follow an animal trail and notice these "digital" pressure releases.

You will begin to see the thought of, for instance, a gait shift or a direction change, one or two steps before the actual shift occurs. Like us, there is often a moment between the thought and the action. These thoughts are readily seen in the tracks. Once we begin to factor these details into our reading of a track, it truly begins to speak. The animal comes to life before us, and a sense of flow and change begins to come through. This is how we can "become" the animal.

A critical distinction can be made at this level. If all parts of a track work as a whole, the pressure releases within the toes are just part of the whole step. They are coordinated and tie together. But if one or two toes show distortions that are not supported by the rest of the track, it may have to do with a separate thought or action.

Micro Movement: Thoughts and Feelings

With micro pressure releases, subtleties such as hesitations, surprise, responses to changing conditions, and events around the animal, as well as its internal state of mind and physical health, are reflected and recorded in the tracks. All of these dynamic physiological processes are translated into the way the feet press into the ground, vibrating, shuddering, compensating, and making extremely small weight adjustments. The details are in the floor of the track itself, expressed in tiny ridges, valleys, and domes.

Be aware that all of this is taking place in tracks—but this level goes far beyond the scope of this overview of pressure releases. You can go as far as your interest will carry you! But remember, it could take years just to absorb what we've discussed here, so relax and take your time with it. Never let yourself get frustrated. Sit back and let your unconscious perceptions do the work. Each small victory, each small step forward, will excite you and fuel your progress toward bringing the tracks to life and connecting with the animals who made them.

June 2017

The Baseline Symphony

Baseline is one of the most important concepts in tracking and nature awareness. Every animal has its baseline behavior and gait. Nature itself has a baseline. But in practice, baseline is elusive and hard to define, and that is exactly why it is such a fascinating and useful concept.

The problem with baseline is that there is no such thing! It is normal but ever shifting, timeless yet never the same. Baseline is a constantly changing state, adjusting in response to time of day, weather, season, recent history, local animal and plant cycles, and endless other variables. But for any one individual, species, or location, at any one moment, there is a baseline.

The "baseline symphony," the natural sounds and movements of animal life, particularly birdcall and song, can be charted throughout the day for any area and season. Morning and evening are usually the busiest and loudest times, and midnight and midday are usually the quietest. This will vary depending on weather and season. In Point

Reyes, the fog and wind have strong effects on animal activity, often suppressing typical dawn behavior, delaying it until better conditions later in the day. Feeding activity here is often most fervent in the sweet spot after the damp morning fogs start to burn off and the day begins to warm, before the consequent winds begin to pick up.

It can be useful to chart the baseline symphony in any new area over a twenty-four-hour period, recording the intensity of calls and movement in a particular location as they rise and fall. Doing this in one spot over the seasons provides a graph of the dynamics of animal life during the year.

Understanding what is normal for any moment gives us a very important key: a way to read disruptions, such as a predator on the prowl. In the case of a bobcat out on the hunt, for instance, birds will often raise a loud alarm and gather to "mob" the cat, perching nearby, looking down, and calling loudly. But when a Cooper's hawk is on the hunt, birds will suddenly go silent and hide quickly under cover. This absence of calls, the "tunnel of silence," is a major disruption of baseline.

Another aspect of baseline is the way each animal normally moves. This can be readily seen in track patterns and bird flight patterns. Each animal has a preferred baseline gait that arises from the morphology of the animal and its role in the habitat. Every species occupies a different habitat niche, a different "job," which is a defining characteristic of a species. Its gait reflects the most efficient bio-mechanical way to move for its purposes within that niche.

Baseline gait for a coyote is a trot, for a bobcat a walk. Baseline for a vole is a trot, but for a mouse it is a bound. Baseline for a skunk is a lope, but for an opossum it is a walk or trot. For a horse it is a lope or gallop. In birds, baseline flight for a red-tailed hawk is a soar; for a woodpecker it is a bounding, undulating pattern of flight; for a duck it is a fast, beeline, powered flight. Of course, each animal can and does travel in a variety of ways, but the baseline is the most common movement under normal conditions. This is one of the great keys to tracking and understanding animal behavior.

Any time an animal moves out of baseline, something has influenced it. Looking for that influence will immerse us in that animal's life. Following a trail and trying to "live into" the movements recorded in the tracks can quickly pull us into the fabric of nature, responding to the same things the animal we are trailing was responding to.

Reading the infinite variations in baseline, as we trail an animal, brings that animal to life, and this is what we love the most about tracking. For instance, as a coyote trots down a beach on its nightly patrol, it constantly shifts and shudders in response to the world around it: the scents on the wind, the sounds and vibrations nearby and distant, the movements of birds. All of these things will influence its gait as it slows down, speeds up, looks around, quickly turns, or shifts its weight and balance. It will repeatedly change from a left side-trot to a right side-trot, to an easy lope, slowing down to a walk as it nears some object, then taking off again in a wild scramble before settling into a trot again. All of these movements can be read in its tracks and compared against baseline.

With these things in mind, I recently followed one of the craziest coyote trails I've ever seen. This coyote had come out of a thicket and emerged through a pinch-point between a steep slope and the edge of a pond. It then trotted across open sand toward a basin near concentrated rodent habitat. For no apparent reason that I could see, it suddenly burst into a dash across the sand in a wild series of gyrating leaps.

COYOTE DANCE

The trail contained every possible gait: rapid shifts from gallop to walk to trot, with double and triple pressure releases in each footstep, and a stretch with a wild series of left-side lopes jumping over to right-side lopes, back and forth, slapping feet spraying sand to all sides, then finally dashing off in a gallop for several more long strides, only to suddenly pivot and trot back to inspect a bobcat scat it had rushed past.

I think the only quality of coyote baseline was the constant change of gaits. If a trot would be considered the most baseline movement for a coyote, then most of the trail I followed was out of baseline, yet still characteristic of coyote. It is fun to conjecture what happened here, but it was truly a "dancing coyote." It is hard for me to imagine how they can slap their feet on the ground to spray sand out to the right and left even while they are powering forward, but they commonly do in moments of wild abandon.

I usually associate that kind of coyote dancing with courtship, but I didn't see any evidence of pairing. Could it be part of claiming a new territory? I did not see much in the way of marking behavior, like scratch-scenting, either. But the way it carefully inspected other scats was suggestive. I've seen this same crazy trail pattern several times since. It is probably the signature movement of a single individual, perhaps a coyote who just happens to have an extra playful personality. This is part of the coyote mystique, a reason why they are so revered in native culture. They are so crazy, and so intelligent, that they remind us uncannily of ourselves.

The best way to get a sense of real baseline is to simply sit somewhere for a while. Pick a nice spot where birds are active, where you might see some deer, where water or good shelter is nearby. If you sit quietly for twenty or thirty minutes, most of the animal life will settle into normal activity. That means, for the most part, feeding. In spring and summer, it involves claiming territory and building nests or dens. In fall it's about fattening up, and in winter it involves courtship.

After being still for a while, you will begin to sense the overall hum of life in its steady state. It is dynamic and changing, but there is a steadiness in it. Everyone is doing their job, staying out of trouble and getting on with life. There is an undeniable sweetness, something about the way it operates as it was designed to do, something that can easily be brought back and re-established in other parts of our lives. Just as the feeling of haste itself can be used as a reminder, or "trigger," to slow down and relax, so the experience of nature returning to baseline can help us recognize when we have become stressed and remind us to return to our own baseline.

April 2014

Love Letters in the Sand

It was mid-winter courting season, and the coyotes were kicking up their heels. I recently followed a trail of a pair of them across the sands of Limantour Beach. They had been loping along a few feet apart, matching each other's movements stride for stride, covering hundreds of yards in that ground-gobbling gait they love. The tracks drew together and almost merged, one close behind the other, when the lead abruptly swerved to the right, closely followed by its mate. They ran around in perfect parallel circles about ten feet in diameter and a foot apart, kicking sand out right and left in wild, celebratory abandon, finally shooting off in their original direction at a fast gallop, exuberant, picking up speed, strides growing with each bound.

In a way, the resulting pattern of tracks looked like a giant ribbon tied in a bow. The story in the tracks was vivid. The joy, the camaraderie, the implicit sense of security, and the profound "belongingness" of the coyotes were clear. Coyotes in love! Just like our domestic dogs, these canines express their joy with their body language. The tracks of courting coyotes display the same enthusiastic care that your wiggly dog will show when you come home at the end of the day. Like any animal who expresses itself so physically, coyotes are also, correspondingly, extremely keen observers. They note every detail, every blink of an eye or tremble of a muscle, making them seem almost like mind readers. It is always a profound experience to encounter a coyote in its home territory and watch how their glance assesses your very inner being.

Midwinter is an ideal time to see coyotes. The landscapes are more open, and the coyotes are not as secretive as usual. I sighted a pair as I walked along the top of the bluff at Railroad Point, at the foot of Tomales Bay, one evening not long ago. After I approached the edge of the bluff, in the gathering darkness, I glimpsed them down on the old railroad bed near the edge of the marsh, fifty feet below and three or four hundred feet ahead, smoothly trotting alongside each other, one slightly ahead, both moving away from me.

I spied the coyotes the moment my head rose over the horizon, but instantly both of them jerked their heads around in a sharp glance over their shoulders and looked directly up at me without breaking stride. That penetrating glance startled me, even from that distance. They turned back as one, and with no further reaction, continued trotting along together and disappeared into the thickets. In one simple coordinated act, they expressed a depth of connection with each other—one might even say a commitment—that said more than words ever could about social relations in the canine.

I've been marveling ever since at their tremendous level of awareness and the sense that they used each other to expand their field of perception. I've been wondering: how they could have known I was up there on the bluff, above and behind them as I was? There was no wind to carry my scent. I was very quiet. It was nearly dark. Yet it was as if they had expected me.

The answer to this question involves some keys to the whole idea of nature awareness—in particular, bird language and coyote teaching. I suspect that the coyotes were using their understanding of birdcalls and movement, expressions of alarm. I think the ducks told them I was up there.

Let me explain a little: bird language is an important branch of awareness. Tom Brown always said that in the Apache language, tracking and awareness were the same word. The definition didn't parse out a focus on footprints from observation in general. They saw tracking more holistically and dynamically.

The same goes for bird language and tracking. Bird language refers to the reactions of birds (and all animals, really) to what is happening around them while they are busy with their lives. Birds in particular constantly communicate with each other through songs, calls, and movements. They are extremely astute observers and listeners of the environment; the landscape plays them like musical instruments as their language conveys detailed and constantly updated information to each other about their surroundings. It is one of their key survival skills. Knowing how birds call and move in regard to relevant events allows us to read the landscape beyond the limits of our direct perceptions. The alarms in particular spread out in concentric rings around any disturbance, much like ripples in a pool.

The coyote, one of the greatest masters of awareness, knows this. This is the coyote's great gift to us. Native Americans recognized this long ago, emulated it, and honored it as coyote teaching, a style of instruction that uses the art of asking questions to stimulate deeper curiosity and elevate awareness.

In times before guns, birds and animals lived much closer to people. Native people could see that the coyote watched them and probed their thoughts and patterns, always curious, always looking for blind spots and advantages—hence their characterization as tricksters.

They understood that the coyote lived in the present, always assessing immediate conditions. They recognized that the coyote was teaching them to be in the moment, and how precious, how sacred, it is to be so attuned to everything going on around you. They knew how critical awareness is for safety and survival, but they also experienced what a powerful salve awareness is for a troubled mind. To be conscious of the incredible, miraculous beauty and interwoven complexity of the world around us is the coyote's gift. When we learn these things, we become connected with our world, and this brings a powerful feeling of joy and happiness.

Those coyotes below the bluff probably sensed a ripple in the patterns of sound and movement among the evening sparrows, towhees, and wrentits, who were sweeping in waves down the hill ahead of me toward roosting spots in the thickets, hinting at my direction. But I suspect that the ducks swimming in the channels along the shoreline of the marsh were the biggest giveaway. These ducks, so hyper-vigilant and wary of hunters (with guns or teeth), immediately swim directly away from a hiker, farther from shore. The more distant ducks move first, having had the first view. Their calls express stress or they stop calling altogether, shifting into a wary silence—a silent alarm that quickly alerts their neighbors. The ducks closest to shore pick up this ripple of alarm and, nervous, react quickly when the hiker appears. The coyote knows this.

Those coyotes were probably generally aware of my presence already. I had been walking around for an hour or so; they might have seen me earlier, possibly on the alert for clues about my location as they sneaked around the edges of my concentric rings on their way to their evening rendezvous. Something in all of this told both of them instantly when I appeared. In typical coyote fashion, having already processed all of this, they were not very concerned about me. I was keeping a low profile, blending in and moving smoothly. They had already categorized me as a non-threat.

Besides, they were coyotes in love, on their way to the evening gathering with friends. They certainly weren't going to let me disrupt their singing session, their chance to celebrate another day of life, and an evening hunt around the edges of the marsh.

December 2008

Touching the Buzzard

I was sitting at the top of Mount Wittenberg with my friend, Michele, one afternoon last summer, resting from the hike up and taking in the view of the Farallon Islands at the horizon of the Pacific Ocean, when a young turkey vulture swept over. He flew in from the east, into the wind, wove a couple circles through the clumps of small fir trees, and then abruptly landed on a gravelly little knob about thirty feet away from us.

This unexpected landing surprised us. We stayed very still, watching as he settled down and began pecking at the gravel, apparently unaware of us, probably refilling the grit in his craw. After a few moments, he turned to face the light breeze, stood up straight, unfurled his wings—huge at such a close distance—and held them fully outstretched. He settled into this pose, almost a meditative state. As he seemed in no hurry to leave, I took advantage of this opportunity to see how close I could get to him.

I eased into a tracker state of mind, consciously slowing myself down, breathing more slowly and widening my vision and awareness. I took a deep breath and shifted into an accepting attitude and an empty mind—the sacred space—ready for whatever might occur. Asking my friend to be as still as she could, I began to crawl very, very slowly toward the buzzard, at a stalking pace, one slow shift of hand or foot at a time, all smooth and fluid. It took about a quarter of an hour to cover the short distance—about two feet per minute—until I was within a foot of this carrion eater. He kept glancing at me out of the corner of his eye and then looking away, as if he were totally unconcerned, and continued to hold his wings out wide, dangling the tips, by now only inches away.

I looked closely at him, albeit with peripheral vision, not wanting to make him nervous with a direct stare. Up close, a vulture is a huge bird. With a six-foot span, his wings, impressive and gorgeous, displayed the perfectly shaped airfoil curve born of gliding on the winds, sweeping up canyons, and circling in thermal updrafts where he and his relations gather each evening, rising in the warm air columns before dispersing in long glides to their roosting areas. His dark brown feathers, long and broad, shimmered with an underlying teal iridescence. His head, not completely red, indicated a juvenile. He was beautiful and fastidiously clean.

I began talking to him in a calm and gentle voice, admiring him without being too direct. I made some polite conversation for a while, and when the time seemed right, I reached out and touched his wing. He shuddered a little, looked askance again, but left his wing outstretched. I began to stroke his outermost wing feathers. I continued talking to him in very low tones, telling stories of how highly I thought of him and what a fine afternoon it was. I avoided saying anything untrue, wanting to convey the proper intentions.

Evolutionary history has made animals highly aware of intent, especially of predators, and they have developed a complex web of alerts to draw attention to any threat. None of their calls or their silences, or their patterns of movement, is random. Insects, birds, and mammals are in a constant state of awareness and conversation, paying casual but critical attention to any disruptions to the normal state.

There is a constant vibrational hum of awareness in nature, and it settles into a beautiful baseline symphony when all is well and safe, everyone going about his or her business. The sounds and movements are very much like background music, almost taken for granted. But any hunting predator, any intent to harm, too much mental focus, or just a simple lack of awareness, can send crashing alarms through this web. Like throwing a rock into the middle of a pond, the disruption sends ripples in all directions. The hum in the baseline is the sum of all these ripples, spreading from all directions with varying intensity. All animals are attuned to these ripples, to the body language of neighboring animals and calls that reflect disruption. But we can learn to move in a way that fits in, bypassing this alarm system.

It starts with calming down. It is not so much a matter of masking intent as creating a different kind of intent and living in that state of mind. There is what I can only call a sacred state that I touch when I embrace this interconnectedness of all things. It is a state of deep love and compassion, the ongoing Buddhism of the natural world, you could say. It is a feeling of relief that can bring me almost to tears when I truly feel it. It is the recognition of intrinsic brotherhood with animals, that which hunter-gatherers called "all my relations." By relaxing into that state of mind, I leave intentions behind and simply live gratefully in the moment: this is when good things begin to happen.

During my slow crawl toward this turkey vulture, I arrived at a surprising state of presence, simply there: no purpose, no schedule, just a part of the fabric. Yet at the same time, I felt aware, all my senses heightened. I was drinking everything in.

The vulture eyed me with the deep wisdom and dignity appropriate to his ancient, vital, and metaphorical profession: an agent of transformation, eater of the dead. He held his ground and let me touch him. I stroked his wing another time or two, noting the dryness, stiffness, and strength. The vulture continued to stare at me closely. Inwardly, I could hardly believe this was happening, face to face with this giant bird. It was enough for me. I eased off and very slowly crawled back to my friend, both of us amazed at what had just happened. Nature had offered a gift. An aura of the magic of having become completely present in such an unexpected situation with a wild animal still hung in the air, a lesson offered and taken.

We can employ such lessons in other areas of our lives and witness equally magical results. Surprising things will happen when living in this state of mind, sometimes things I am not quite prepared for, but always good. It is an amazing skill to learn, but in truth, there is nothing difficult or mystical about it. This way of being is as natural to us as it is to a sparrow or a buzzard, except that we forget about it and it atrophies from disuse. When we do remember it, we find that we enter a world of great joyfulness, and a powerful magnetic attraction arises between that world and ourselves.

As I relaxed and began to return to a more normal human reality with my friend, the buzzard finally drew in his wings. And hopped toward us. We watched, holding our breath, as he walked up and poked around. He approached me, pecking at my feet. That sharp bill made me a little apprehensive, but I slowly reached around, stroked his back, and began to talk to him again, telling stories. He seemed to enjoy it, so I went a little further, curious and amazed. Eventually, I was grasping his shoulders, rocking him back and forth. We were old buddies. We played for another ten minutes, while the world paused.

Wild animals seem to love it when you successfully quiet your mind and enter their world. They become playful and curious, drawn to us, enjoying our powerful aura once we feel safe to them. It is almost as if they are celebrating our return to the fold as we become invisible like normal animals instead of so characteristically human, so obvious and out of place, as if we finally came home.

Finally, Michele and I stood up to head back toward the trailhead far below, but our little friend was reluctant for us to leave. It was as if he knew how much trouble I was struggling with at the time and wanted to accompany me on my difficult journey through some life transitions. But I gently shooed him back into his own world, the world he belongs to.

March 2008

False Spring: January and February

As I write on this winter morning, the dawn sun is streaming into my living room, the sky is clear, the wetlands below are at high tide, and the surface of the water barely stirs in the light breezes. In the trees and underbrush, the birds, from crows and gulls to jays and sparrows, call in an easy baseline chorus. The day has begun, pleasant and warm. It is a mid-winter pause, False Spring if you will, a chance for the Earth to catch its breath and relax for a moment before the next cold, rainy cycle begins.

There is brilliance in this plan, and paying attention to it can help us navigate occasional feelings of sadness that the short days and cold nights can bring. It is all cyclical. Life, nature, our emotions, and our souls were created out of the seasonal cycles, the serendipity of a tilted rotational axis as the earth revolves around the sun. The rotational axis tilts twenty-three degrees from the axis of our orbit around the sun. That's a lot! And it is the cause of the annual progression of the earth's seasons.

Once the fall rains brought an end to the long dry season and set the clock into motion, there was an almost frantic flurry of growth and activity. There was an exuberance, a joyful abandon, in this pulse of life and action, even as the days grew shorter and temperatures dropped.

Winter brings heavy rain for days at a time, followed by long cold nights and frozen mornings. The mice and gophers snuggle down in their little balls of dried grasses, just as I keep close to the woodstove and the couch. The world pauses. We naturally go inward. One eye glances back at good times past, while the other looks forward to warm days ahead.

Hunter-gatherers, closer to the elements than we are now, lived more in tune with these rhythms. They drew closer together in the long, cold nights, turning inward for purification and healing and re-telling the stories that carried the body of their wisdom and guided their lives. They repeated timeless rituals of gratitude and prayer to celebrate the season. They lived off the harvests of fall and prepared their tools for the coming spring, while the winter storms raged. But often in early January, the winter relents, and a few days of sun take the hard edge off.

Whenever the weight of winter is lifted for a moment, there is a burst of animal activity everywhere. A short respite from the arctic air streams shows how lively the world really is underneath the shrouds of frost. Take a brief walk along the shorelines. Where the dunes were blank slates two or three weeks ago, animals all hunkered down in a winter torpor, they are suddenly speckled with thousands of mouse tracks. Walk across a grassy, south-facing hillside and notice the explosion of new gopher tailings.

All across the landscape, the warmer nights from the last week spark an abrupt awakening. The foragers—skunks in particular, but opossums and raccoons as well—emerge from short-term semi-hibernation for double-duty activity, crisscrossing the landscape to fill up on new plant growth and insect hatches while searching for mates. For a month or so, skunks were nowhere to be found; suddenly their tracks are everywhere. The pause in winter is a time of intense social activity for them, in perfect harmony with the cycle of the seasons, everything timed for birthing in the generosity of the spring and childrearing in the abundance of summer.

While the deer have already mated, now separating into male and female winter groups, coyotes are in the full swing of their courting season, re-establishing social bonds and hierarchies in their intense musical midnight gatherings. Soon they will seek safe denning sites for their mid-spring litters. Meanwhile, they seize any opportunity between storms to roam the borders of their territories, quick to renew scent posts that mark their boundaries.

Bobcats, in contrast to the canines yet in the same seasonal patterns, are pairing up too, in the peripheries. While the females are locking down their relatively small and well-defined home territories and denning and daybed locations, the males are roaming farther, surveying the land for prey and mates, just as their ancestors have for millions of years.

Foxes, too, are ready to seize any break in the weather. Their habits, like their tracks, fall between canine and feline; they are very social, not solitary, but furtive and close to cover. They find a nice umbrella of safety from the threat of coyote predation by moving closer to human habitation. As a result, sometimes the easiest places to find fox dens and observe the families are right in some of the neighbors' back yards, particularly where wild thickets are nearby. Like coyotes, they are quick to use breaks between storm systems to forage and re-scent their boundaries.

So, just as my local animal relatives do, I'm letting myself be drawn outside on these wonderful, almost summery days between storms. The darkest, coldest days, from the solstice to early January, have passed. Sometimes, in the dark of winter, I struggle with cynicism that can be exaggerated by all the Christmas marketing of good cheer and the appearance of love so jarringly tied to objects and sales. These feelings fade when the false spring makes a surprise appearance, and thoughts become more hopeful. These soft days before the spring are gifts to be treasured. Answer the call! Get outside with some friends. The moment is waiting for you to embrace it.

May 2016

Signs of Life

How do you track where there are no tracks? It is an important question: most locations have little soft substrate, and a good track can be hard to find. But animals leave many kinds of marks—the effects of their activities—that can be read and interpreted just like tracks. These signs are as important as tracks in re-animating the world and bringing a landscape to life.

Sign tracking is an aspect of nature awareness that is often overlooked when people think of tracking, but it can open doors to the secret worlds of nature even more profoundly than the study of footprints. Sign tracking refers to all the indications animals leave of their presence as they move through their daily rhythms and routes. It includes feeding signs, scat, rubs, chews, beds, nests, burrows, trails, runs, pass-throughs, foraging digs, probes, feathers, bones, territorial and social markers, and more. We are often surrounded by signs, but they can nevertheless be very subtle and hard to see—

much less to interpret, even to a trained eye.

Paying attention at this level is unfamiliar to most of us, and it takes a while to become comfortable with it. Eventually, when our awareness sharpens and becomes a living practice, the joy of watching nature come alive creates an excitement that carries us along tirelessly. But for me, at first, when I was sorting out difficult mysteries, I would hit a wall of tiredness, even irritation. Awareness at this level was unfamiliar and exhausting. It required a shift out of the schedule-driven world I usually occupied.

It takes me a while to slow my inner clock, to fully arrive and begin opening my senses, to see and hear and smell what's around me. I love hiking and covering distance over the landscape, but sign tracking requires letting go of the desire to reach a destination. It is a shift from being a tourist in nature to becoming a part of nature. This is a visceral shift, a physical and mental process, and, like slowing down a car, it takes a little time.

But with patience and the supportive curiosity of like-minded friends, I make that shift, let more of the world in, and suddenly find myself energized by the comprehensive story emerging around me, connecting with both the world and something deeply satisfying inside.

The other day I went out with a couple of friends to Bear Valley, the park's headquarters and where a number of trails begin, to test sign tracking possibilities in the forests and fields there. Our goal was to find some recent antler-rubbing locations in the willow thickets. We parked the car and scanned the picnic grounds for a while before getting out. The first thing we noticed was a group of acorn woodpeckers busily working in the tops of the tall firs at the edges of the forest, noisily calling, swirling around, in the full swing of social activity. Gray squirrels a little farther back were jumping from limb to limb, circling up and down the trunks, and making occasional forays across the forest floor. Flickers and Steller's jays were landing below the oaks, pecking at the ground.

We strolled over to the tall firs, amazed to see them riddled, base to crown, with thousands of three-quarter-inch holes, almost all filled with tightly wedged acorns. It was quite a sight! This is one of several "granary trees" in the area, the work of woodpecker colonies that must be hundreds, if not thousands, of generations old. Their raucous calls fill the air—"Bud-dabba! Bud-dabba!"—sounding remarkably like Woody Woodpecker. They work continuously, resetting the acorns as they dry and shrink so they stay tightly wedged, harder for other birds and rodents to steal.

Looking up into the huge old bay trees closer to the creek, we saw that one or two of them were covered with tens of thousands of small, quarter-inch holes drilled in close parallel rows around the trunks and branches. These are ancient feeding trees for sapsuckers who tap into the cambium layer and let the little wells fill. What would make one bay tree more desirable than another? Better taste or sweetness? Better location for trapping insects in the oozing sap?

Soon we shifted our attention to the forest floor. Mammals work in specific strata in the ground, much the way bird species occupy different height zones in trees. When you examine the ground carefully, you can see a history in the debris layer, the top inch or two on the forest floor, reaching back several years: new leaves at the very top, decomposed leaves at the bottom in the process of becoming soil, a highly variable layer of new soil underneath that, eventually giving way to mineral sub-soils. It is a complex zone exploited by many opportunists, in a range of digging patterns.

One of the first things I noticed on the ground under the bay trees was a pattern of disruptions in the leafy top layer from the hoof-tips of the deer who regularly pass through, nibbling on fresh forbs and new-fallen nuts. A few leaves were tossed in little clusters at each step, but there was no apparent digging in them.

Moving slowly, we examined the more-exposed ground under the oak trees, finding numerous smooth-rimmed little holes, ground-ant nests—wiped clean by the long, sticky, probing tongue of the flickers—and several small diggings from scrub jays hunting for insects. With a sideways flick of the head, the jays had thrown small scatterings of soil, about two inches wide, to the side.

These digs were not as deep or conical as the numerous three- to four-inch-wide holes we found a little further on, both under the trees and along the grassy slopes, the signs of skunks hunting for insects.

We found a few small skunk scats along these foraging routes, crumbly and full of the tan-colored remnants of their favorite prey, the Jerusalem cricket.

In between these two scales of digs were little flat-bottomed holes with the leafy surface debris pulled aside in a small apron, the result of the gray squirrels foraging for their cached nuts.

The more we slowed down, the more we found. As we moved toward the creek, into the brushy margins, we discovered woodrat and deer mouse nests in piles of branches and the hollowed-out trunks of the old trees, the methods of nest building and shapes and sizes of scat differentiating rat from mouse. There were signs of feeding, too. Bay nuts are a prized food for rodents, as well as the jays and quail. What is of interest to a tracker is the way the nuts have been penetrated, since each mammal and bird has its own particular method of opening them to extract the food. We found shells with the telltale incisor nibbles of rodents, shells with broken edges revealing that a bird had pecked its way in, and some shells completely crushed, indicating that deer had munched them.

We circled around through the oak groves and toward the meadows. Acorns on the ground can be quite revealing; like bay nuts, many different animals feed on them, from squirrels, mice, rats, and deer, to woodpeckers, jays, crows, and turkeys, each one leaving characteristic marks and patterns in the remnant shells and the disruptions on the forest floor. We found other signs in the area, too: small hairs from raccoons and opossums that had rubbed against branches, as well as snips and tears on leaves and buds, the rodents leaving sharply cut ends while deer clamp and tear, fraying the edges.

It went on, expanding the more we looked. We were surrounded by a record of overwhelming activity, an ever-changing interplay between animals, plants, and the landscape.

One of my favorite discoveries was a series of little gouges on the top of some horizontal oak branches, which proved to be sap wells created by gray squirrels. Like the sapsuckers that pecked into the bay trees at the beginning of our walk, these tree dwellers have also learned to tap this food source by chewing to the cambium layer, letting the sap run and fill the wells. Then the sun evaporates the water in the sap, greatly concentrating the sugar content. These wells are located on branches with good sun exposure. The gouges are part of a system of chew marks that can be generations old, claiming certain branches and trees as a personal territory for that individual squirrel. It speaks of an immensity of time that for some reason brings a deep laughter boiling up out of my depths.

You just have to ask, how did those squirrels learn this? Just how complex is the relationship between animals and the world? How much more is right there under our noses if only we can see it?

Close to the meadow edges, we passed through a patch of mole works—surface tunnels and small domed mounds—where they forage for underground insects as well as earthworms. These mole diggings begin to give way to the larger, sideways-pushed gopher mounds in the drier soils further out in the fields.

Down the trail and into the meadows, we found little groups of matted-down hollows in the grass, the resting spots of deer. Touching them, these lie-spots were noticeably warmer than the surrounding ground, revealing that we had probably just disturbed a family. The outline of the deer is apparent in the lie, its head and rear distinctive, and the punchy hoof marks tell the story of how a deer stands up from the resting position, up on its rear hooves first, then its front wrists and finally its front hooves.

This landscape was coming to life. There was a lot going on here! We moved on, encountering bobcat and coyote scat along the trail, full of telltale fur and bones (gophers on the menu lately), the very pattern of placement of the scats telling its own story. In particular, there were the typical bobcat scat collections, built up over months, marking important side routes to hunting locations.

Continuing our journey, we soon discovered some much larger holes, eight to ten inches deep with vertically oblong openings, and twenty-four-inch throw-mounds out to the sides. Coyotes had clearly been hunting here, digging out gopher and vole nests, locating the active nests by sound, digging with front feet equipped with strong toenails, and pulling the soil out between their back legs in typical dog fashion. Balls of dried grasses from the rodent nests can often be found in these throw-mounds.

Another type of dig commonly found in coyote territory is a scent-scrape. They will regularly renew territorial markings, especially after rains dilute the odors. Vigorous, long, deep scratches with both their back and front feet will gouge the ground over a five-foot circle. While scratching, scent glands in their feet rub the scent into the ground.

Walking further out into the back corners of the fields, we might find digs on yet another scale: holes two or three feet deep, with four-foot throw-mounds often full of large rocks, much larger than a coyote or fox could dig. If we are lucky, we might find deep grooves in the walls of the holes, the result of the long powerful digging claws of the wide-bodied badgers, who are also hunting gophers out here. Looking at these impressive earthworks, you can see the strength of the badger and the rapid fury of their digging. A badger can dig a hole to disappear into in a matter of minutes.

Amazed, almost mesmerized, we continued in the meadows, finding a couple of bird-kills just beyond the brush, a quail and a killdeer, the feathers coarsely chewed off the way a bobcat would, not plucked like a hawk. The surface of the ground under the thick grass was covered with mazes of vole runs. Small round brush rabbit runs popped up at the base of bramble thickets, the larger runs circling the thickets from the deer feeding on the freshest blackberry leaves.

Finally, our goal—remember that?—drew us toward the willows growing along a small creek close to the main trail, where, sure enough, we found a concentration of battered, frayed, and scraped branches, where bucks had rubbed their antlers during the recent rutting season. It is quite common, especially on trees with soft bark, but still almost as startling as finding a bobcat or mountain lion scratching post deep in a canyon.

It was long thought that the rubbing relieved the itching of their rapidly growing antlers and removed the velvet in preparation for sparring in the rutting season. But a little reflection makes you wonder why the rubbing is so concentrated in one spot, if it is just a mechanical antler-cleaning function. And indeed, recent research shows a far more complex social aspect to this activity. These rubs are visual and olfactory markers that allow does and bucks to assess each other's health and vigor. Deer have scent glands on their faces and foreheads that they are rubbing on the branches. The scent is then transferred to their antlers when they spar with the branches. They spread this scent through the forest when they leave, broadcasting their desirability.

There is some debate that maybe it works the other way: perhaps the bucks are shredding the bark with their antlers *and then* rubbing their scent glands onto the shreds, the better to hold the scent on the branches. And there is at least one more dimension to these deer rubs: the very sound of the thrashing is an indication, a display, of the strength and vigor of the buck. It's something the available does are no doubt noting, but the bucks are paying attention too, part of establishing a social order among the males.

Nature presents us with complexity, often contradicting what we may have read in books, often something we've never even seen or heard about before. These are moments of opportunity. We can file these mysteries away on a little shelf in our minds, where they live while awaiting further information, almost unconscious, but ready to light up quickly when information relevant to the answer appears. You begin to realize that the evolutionary history of wildlife has imbued the slightest signs and activities with complex, multi-layered meanings, and you have been blessed with a glimpse into the web of creation.

February 2010

Scat Anyone?

I have to admit it: I am a scatologist.

Now, I know you probably think that scat is just "you know what." But once you start tracking, it becomes much more than that, and you really begin to forget the "poop" part. Scat is a major sign that animals leave of their presence, diet, range, and activity. Scat can be tracked just as well as footprints, especially where there is little good substrate for clear prints. Scat can give you an idea of what an animal is doing, what it is eating, how it is interacting with other animals, how it is relating to the landscape, how its territory is shaped, where its food sources are, and what food is most abundant at the time. Scat is an incredibly important tool in the quest to understand a landscape.

Every animal leaves scat somewhere, and all of it can be identified and analyzed for information. Insects and other invertebrates leave characteristic scat along with their many signs and trails. Birds and reptiles have similar scats, and their prey or plant food is often readily identifiable. Most carnivorous and omnivorous birds, such as gulls, hawks and herons, leave smooth-walled cough pellets with solid waste materials nicely packaged, which can be easily examined for contents. Each species of rodent has its typical size, shape, color, and usual location of scat, all of which provide immediate clues to their presence and populations.

Location of scat is a primary sign among predators. We often see bobcat, coyote, fox, and even mountain lion scat placed in the middle of our hiking trails, commonly at intersections. These animals are quick to tell us, and each other, of their presence. Just as chew marks are a visual language conveying many layers of information, the same goes with scat placement. Animals are highly aware of it, using it with complex intentions. Bobcats often leave scat at a corner where a side trail leads off a major travel route into a current hunting area, both lightening up before the hunt and leaving a reminder of a good hunting location. Gray foxes are known for precise placement of their scat on slightly raised points on a trail—a rock, a root, or even on top of the scat of another animal, including other foxes. They are also famous for placing their scat on the corners of decks or the edges of steps, claiming your yard as their territory. Coyotes spend less time on trails, since they are often traveling across open country, but will often place a scat on a trail at a crossing point, advertising their presence.

It becomes difficult to just go on a normal walk with trackers. No longer can you simply hike along the Sky Trail on Mount Wittenberg, chatting away, accruing miles. Trackers frequently stop and gather around something on the ground, bending over, looking closely, poking, animatedly talking things over and pointing around them, before moving down the trail again, interest heightened, frequently interrupting conversation to stop and inspect something on the ground again. It gets harder and harder to get from point A to point B. Each scat tells a story begging to be heard. Perhaps this fascination is rooted in our own deep animal history. The contents become a fascination, little bone or feather bits, tufts of hair, fruits, and seeds. They immediately paint a picture of the surrounding countryside. Each scat is communicating a deep story about territorial boundaries, health, social position, reproductive status, and food availability.

As a scatologist, understanding fur and bone structures of various prey species, and the fibrous qualities of local plants, can offer a pretty accurate picture of what an animal is eating, and therefore where and when they are eating. Jaws of rodents often make it through the digestive process, the tooth arrangements immediate identifiers.

On a recent walk near Bear Valley, I picked apart a bobcat scat and found a small cat claw. Then I found what looked like another longer claw. Looking closer, the second "claw" turned out to be a tiny incisor tooth and jaw, with molars, of a vole. The zigzag surface pattern of the molars, small as they are, is typical and unique to voles.

The small claw is a mystery, but it might have been the result of that common habit among predators of eating the young of competitors, perhaps the claw of a newborn bobcat kitten. It is vitally important to view this in the proper way, avoiding anthropomorphic values, with deep respect for patterns of population balance that are so critical in nature.

The Point Reyes National Seashore has one of the most stable and mature bobcat populations in the country. We are seeing a healthy system in action. It is a great gift to observe how an un-violated ecosystem actually works. The bobcat scat around Abbotts Lagoon often reveals the patterns of their seasonal diet shifts, from rodents and rabbits in spring and summer to migrating coots and shorebirds in the fall and winter.

The main lesson that nature keeps impressing on me, as I get ever closer, is simple: they are all eating each other out there! This realization yields a sacred respect when we grasp that this is exactly how it is supposed to be. This is healthy biology in action. This is one of the most profound lessons that can be learned in nature. These are the ancient instructions that our whole living Earth developed in the creation of life. This is how life expresses itself.

The death of one creature in the jaws of another is never an occasion for sadness. It is a moment to celebrate. It is life playing itself exactly as it is supposed to. We often carry a misplaced sympathy for prey animals, but this is a serious mistake, ironically by a species that is a master of violence against itself and of interfering on a colossal, disastrous scale with natural systems. Scat is indeed a voice of the truth in nature.

The study of scat is a rich and rewarding experience. But think about the animals themselves. With their powerful sense of smell, commonly thousands of times sharper than humans, they read far more in a scat than we do. What we consider repugnant odors are primal, sensory libraries of information. This is obvious; most animals sniff scat with great interest. It is hard to imagine all the information that must be available in those scents, the way age, health, reproductive cycles, and mental status of the animal are conveyed in the aromas of digestion and hormones. We can learn to interpret some of this by appearance, the coatings and sheen of scats, as well as by building our own library of odor variations.

Once you begin to realize how much is being said with a scat and how much it can tell you about the surroundings, it becomes a regular part of a walk, part of the tapestry of information that you can gather almost effortlessly, employing nothing more than a curious mind and a sharp eye.

May 2008

Cracking the Egg

When I took my first tracking and awareness classes at Tom Brown's school in New Jersey, Tom began by noting that in the Apache language, tracking and awareness are the same word. It took me a while to understand what this meant. I thought that tracking literally meant following footprints.

Though there are times when a hunter-gather, or a modern nature-loving outdoorsman, will follow tracks, the term "tracking" includes noticing the details around us and assembling the pieces in an ongoing, dynamic realization. This is where nature appreciation meets ancient survival hunting, where immersion in nature truly begins. This kind of tracking is built upon deep knowledge derived from acute observation.

In our tracking club, we have called this various things: "holistic awareness," "bringing the world back to life," "re-animating the world," or simply "awareness tracking." It is a way of walking, of watching the earth and its patterns come to life as we go forth.

Awareness tracking is concerned with weather history, seasonal cycles, landscape and topography, plant and insect patterns, feeding sign, bird movements, and more. With a working knowledge of local animal populations, very small details quickly yield broad insights. A tracker develops a living sense of how animals respond to the progression of days and seasons, where animals live, what territories they occupy, and when they are active. When we approach nature this way, it is like cracking open a magical egg and watching as endless surprises issue forth.

The smallest observations spur the process. On a walk near the beach one winter morning, I find a feather on the ground. A quick scan reveals a nearby cluster of feathers, under a lupine bush: a bird kill. The location and the scattered pattern are not typical of raptor predation, so I suspect a mammal. With their light brown edges, the feathers are from a quail, and with that in mind, glancing around, I notice quail tracks covering the dusty gopher mounds surrounding this spot. Hmm. The presence of many active gophers implies healthy, growing grass and other small mammals such as voles and brush rabbits. Sure enough, the half-tunnel vole runs threading the grasses look recently used, and there are numerous little four-inch tunnels that brush rabbits make to move out from the cover of lupines to browse on grasses.

In fact, I'm beginning to notice that this particular area is much richer and greener than the surrounding countryside. With its southern aspect and its bowl shape, the plant community has not entered such a deep winter pause. It is a warm wrinkle, an oasis in the landscape, with more insects and birds in the air.

White-crowned sparrows are busy in the surrounding brush. I realize that a scattered pattern on the ground—overlaid by quail tracks and almost unnoticeable—is an assemblage of sparrow tracks, from their foraging earlier in the morning before the quail. It might imply that seeds have dropped to the ground, mixing with newly sprouted grasses after recent rains.

Now, looking carefully at the wing remains of the bird carcass, I see that the primary feathers have been chewed off rather roughly, not like the clean slice of a coyote's sharp-edged side teeth, the carnassials. A search soon turns up a fresh bobcat scat, surface sheen beginning to dull, full of brown feathers that look suspiciously like quail coverlets. Things are adding up. The scat also contains brown-tipped gopher fur, and, sure enough, jawbone fragments in the scat are from a gopher. This is clearly a productive hunting area right now.

As I scan the rough ground, my eyes see with this new intelligence and pick up otherwise nearly invisible details. The ground under one shaded edge of a lupine is still damp. Bingo! There is a track: a couple of small circular impressions, the toes and part of the heel pad of a bobcat. It has weathered slightly, puffed up a little, a few loose soil grains in the floor giving it a time scale. Given the still, cool days and nights lately, it would have aged slowly, so the track is probably more than a day old, which matches the apparent age of the quail wing: recent, but not from today. The placement of the bobcat scat, just off the hiking trail, shows that this cat uses the hiking trail to travel and turns off here to hunt. The cat is probably working a larger territory and comes through every few nights.

Meanwhile, I've noticed that the sparrows have suddenly gone silent, and their quiet gives me an uneasy feeling. Quickly I turn, in time to see a marsh hawk, the northern harrier, cruising just above the tops of the shrubs in the open chaparral nearby, with that wonderful tilting, slow flight offering another indication of the fecundity of this particular hunting area. An old coyote bush snag nearby has scratch marks and whitewash on the branches, signs that it is regularly used as a perch. Inspecting the ground around the base of the shrub, I find raptor cough pellets full of little caches of tiny bones and teeth in their fur-cushioned casings, with tooth patterns characteristic of the vole.

All of this has taken but a few minutes. The egg is cracking. The further I go, the better the story gets. With each step, I'm more deeply enmeshed.

January 2012

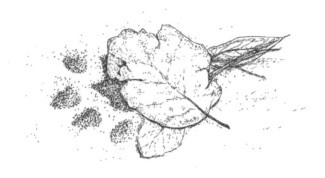

Walking Through Walls

My friend and I are walking together along a familiar trail, excited about the prospects ahead. The day is alive, sunny, but a sharp, cold spring wind has picked up, coming in off the ocean from the northwest. We park the car, jump out, get organized, and head down the sandy trail through the chaparral. At first our minds are spinning in the usual circles of haste and distraction. The wind drives us farther back into the well-worn ruts of our endless inner conversations, not really listening to each other, not noticing where we are and what is around us. It was a busy morning, hard to break away. We arrived, but we are not present.

But as trackers committed to awareness, we have a few tools at our disposal—in fact, some of the oldest in the human tool kit, and they are quickly called forth by the gentle voices of nature: the sound of the breeze through the grass, or a distant birdcall. Distraction itself can also be a catalyst; once you begin to practice awareness, the jabber of a distracted mind seems to get louder and can be used to remind us to make a shift. Without a word, we respond to these signals, slowing down together. At first it is an inner slowing, a slight change in our minds, but then we physically slow down as well, each step a little shorter, a little quieter. We remember our breathing and shift into long, slow, rhythmic breaths. The more present we become, the less apparent our presence is.

As we stroll along, quieting ourselves, we widen our vision and hearing, the kaleidoscope of sensory information growing richer, the riot of smells growing stronger, and the symphony of sounds growing louder. Colors intensify. Details sharpen. Patterns emerge, a sense of the whole context in which we are immersed. We walk more softly, moving together. We let the world ahead adjust to our approach, instead of charging into it. We begin moving in response to our surroundings, sometimes stopping and listening for no apparent reason, before resuming our walk. The landscape plays us. We are becoming an expression of the landscape.

What is this joy we begin to feel, this sense of being bathed in light? We are entering a different world. This is the place in our hearts that laughs with delight whenever we return to it. We just walked through a wall, as slick as any science fiction character, and re-assembled on the other side. We passed beyond our spinning minds and back into the present moment.

We come to a wide, protected area in the trail, covered in a texture of dust and debris and a maze of small, faint, crisscrossing tracks. Down on hands and knees, we pick it apart, trying to see who has been here and what stories it has to tell. I begin to hit my walls again. My enthusiasm wanes in the face of confusion, and I feel frustrated. My mind protests. How can I possibly sort this out? I'm getting tired. I want my old, familiar ruts. I'm supposed to know things, right? I want names and answers, right now. It is too far out on the edge.

My friend gently points out the faint impression on a small, slightly cracked leaf, a detail I couldn't see from my angle of view, and asks if it might be part of a cat track. Maybe so. I ask how old it might be, given the crispness of the grains of dust pressed into the floor of the print. We consider the soil and the weather. Then he draws my attention to the next track, invisible at first, giving us a sense of scale and stride. More details appear. The tracks awaken. We keep asking questions. The tracks are coming to life. A holographic picture of the animal forms right before our eyes.

Let go of knowing. Ask more questions, the most important tools in the kit! What am I actually looking at? What is going on here? What could this mean? How does this fit with everything else? What else must be here?

He triggered my shift. I take another long slow breath and let it go. I come back to the moment, and the tracks brighten. The little grains of dust look obvious and magnified, while the overall patterns become more apparent. The story emerges. It is like reading a book, like hearing the earth speak. It is startling and astounding.

We have walked through another wall! We are right here, asking questions, absorbing our perceptions, completely engaged. The answering and the knowing can wait till later. Right now we are simply being alive.

June 2008

The Fox

The iconic fox is a mysterious character on the Inverness Ridge. Elusive, quick, alert, beautiful, foxes occupy a special place in our hearts and in our stories. They symbolize awareness, stealth, intelligence, and canniness. Our gray fox, its fur elegantly tinged with rust, small and as invisible as it chooses to be, works in a variety of habitats, skirting the edges of cover or moving quickly and quietly along barely perceptible trails through thickets. It hunts voles, gophers, and insects in open meadows, rabbits in the brush and chaparral, birds and eggs in the willow thickets, and mice in the forests. It forages the seashore and creek edges for crustaceans and harvests a wide variety of plants and fruits throughout the area. With sharp, semi-retractable claws, a mother fox will easily climb an apple tree to knock down fruit for her pups.

While the gray fox is a true American native, the red fox, rare in Point Reyes, is actually an introduced species. Although recent genetic research suggests that remnant populations of native red foxes may exist in isolated pockets of the Rockies and the Sierras, most red foxes in our landscapes are descendants of animals introduced from England. The story of this introduction illuminates characteristics of the native fox while providing a glimpse into an aspect of colonial America's social structure that is somewhat ignored in our history texts.

Early members of the wealthy, land-holding class of the new American colony were accustomed to fox hunting back in the country estates of England. But when they tried it with the local gray foxes, they were disappointed; instead of leading their dogs and horses on wild chases across the countryside, the gray fox quickly climbed into the trees, and the hunt was over. Bummer for the aristocrat, not to mention the fox.

Disappointed in the native fox but committed to the old pastime, the colonists imported and released red foxes from England. As is usually the case with non-native animals (with no natural limits), they soon spread across the landscape and established wild populations that have grown and persisted in North America ever since, to the detriment of many native species.

The "problem" the colonists encountered with the gray fox is that, in many ways, it is half cat. Native Americans recognized this, and commonly had names for the fox that essentially meant "cat-dog." Luckily, the two fox species can survive and tolerate each other, as their niches and morphological characteristics are sufficiently different to avoid direct competition. The gray fox is accustomed to climbing in trees, hunting birds, and foraging fruit. It is a creature of forest and cover, while the red fox leans more toward coyote-like habits, preferring open country like the rolling hills and broad coastlines of England. The red fox is much larger than the gray fox. Its tracks are oval, with visible toenails like a coyote, while gray fox tracks are round like a cat's, with infrequent toenail marks.

An unfortunate difference is that the red fox is much more tolerant of wet habitats and will wade or even swim across tidal channels to reach shorebird nests that the gray fox will not. In tideland restorations around the perimeter of San Francisco Bay, where there are efforts to re-build the clapper rail population, the exotic red fox will hunt beyond the normal range of gray foxes and prey heavily on nesting rails who evolved with the more limited hunting range of the native gray fox. Before the rails were hunted to near extinction for their meat and eggs in the late 1800s, the marshes lining the bay supported millions of rails. Current restorations struggle to protect the re-established populations in the new marshes. One red fox can destroy a whole nascent rail population, so marsh projects require constant vigilance.

Compounding the problem, fur farms in the Central Valley imported and bred red foxes in the early 1900s. Failing farms sometimes released their animals into the landscape, and the red fox became a common wild canine in many parts of the state, eventually reaching the coastline. But here in West Marin, at least, the red fox has not gained a hold. There are only rare anecdotal sightings that were most likely gray foxes with particularly rusty coats. The biggest threat to the gray fox (other than disease) is from coyotes, but these two canines manage to coexist for the most part.

Gray foxes have a unique habit of intentionally depositing their scat on top of other animal scat along trails or precisely placing it on slightly raised rocks or roots. It is a claim of territory, a bold statement for a canine not much bigger than a cat. In yards near the edges of the forest, they will often leave scat pellets on decks or the edges of steps. The mixed omnivorous diet, readily seen in its scat, can lead a tracker directly to the fox's recent foraging areas.

With its retractable claws, furry feet, and direct-registering trot pattern, the gray fox is very quiet on its feet. If a clear track can be found, the heel pad is much smaller than a bobcat's, as if it is tiptoeing. A fox track is usually smaller than a bobcat track, but in dry, loose substrates it can be difficult to tell the difference. However, a wider view of the whole trail pattern reveals the difference. A bobcat trail usually reveals a leisurely, steady pace as the cat patiently walks its regular routes to reach hunting grounds. But the fox typically moves across the open in a zippier, zigzaggy pattern, with many abrupt turns as it follows its nose and ears to patrol its regular foraging routes at a more frenetic pace.

Foxes are always present around Kehoe Beach, often leaving trails along the foredunes in both directions. The cliffs to the north, the dunes to the south, the long marsh, and the creek pouring out onto the beach create just enough habitat and cover for the fox to make a tolerable living. But to the south, Abbotts Lagoon and beyond, where the land is more open and rolling and coyote is king, there are few gray foxes.

Cruising along the base of the wildly eroded sandstone cliffs at Kehoe, the resident fox often stops to check for remnants thrown out of peregrine nests high above the dunes. There is a well-used spot at a high point where the dunes push up against the cliff wall, where it sits to take in the view. I can easily imagine it paying rapt attention, nose up, to the rich odors swirling around, to the patterns of distant sounds as it reads the landscape, probably aware of my approach long before I come into view.

One of the fox's most iconic characteristics is its keen perceptiveness and an almost uncanny intelligence in interpreting what it senses, responding almost before something happens. The fox is an expert at reading the forest or field for alarms and disruptions in baseline activity. This is an aspect of fox awareness that the tracker can tune into and use. The fox seems particularly sensitive to the out-of-context behavior typical of humans, particularly the unsettled mental state we are often so caught up in. Trackers commonly report that when they learn to quiet their minds and harmonize with spirit of nature, the fox begins to reveal itself, almost as if complimenting us for our accomplishment. In this way, the fox can be used as an indicator of how well we are learning to let go of distracting thoughts and be more present in nature.

"Fox-walking" is a term trackers and Native Americans use for a way of moving, silent and relaxed, yet in an extreme state of awareness that animals respond to. We call it "lowering your profile." Your body relaxes, and, with your senses alert and mental energy flowing smoothly, you begin to let the landscape, and everything happening in it, guide and move you.

Instead of projecting your presence outward in all directions, you have brought your profile in to the point that the landscape begins to reach toward you! An animal, such as a fox, who is used to the normally loud profile of a human, can become very curious when someone doesn't match the norm, and can be drawn toward you. Lowering your profile and expanding into full awareness are two of the primary tools of a tracker interested in establishing a deeper connection with nature. It is a way of allowing nature around us to carry on in its normal, undisturbed state, as if we were not there. The fox is the perfect model for this attitude. This is how animals become our teachers.

October 2010

Great Tracks I Have Known

Thinking back over my tracking experiences, there are several individual tracks that stand out clearly for the impact they had on me and the progress they helped me make. Moments like these stand as memorable waypoints in our journey as we become trackers. The lessons they contain can continue teaching us for years.

The first one that comes to mind for me was a single otter track, in a whole set of tracks. I was standing out on Railroad Point greeting the dawn, several years ago, when I heard splashing sounds down on the mudflats. I looked down from the bluff to see a family of otters emerge from the tidal channel and dash across the muddy sandbar to Papermill Creek. They bounded across the open ground, jostling each other as they ran, seeming to crave physical contact. The sound of their feet slapping the mud, multiple sharp wet slaps in fast profusion, remains as clear in my memory as the image of their dash to the creek. I watched them slip into the water and swim upstream, weaving along the far shore until they disappeared in the morning mist.

I ran down to inspect this gift. With the visual image of their movements still in mind, I observed the pattern of their tracks in the mud. Most four-legged mammals have larger front feet than rear because they have to support the greater weight of the chest and head. But otters have the larger back feet unique to animals who swim. Because of their frenetic energy, their gaits and track patterns can be hard to sort out, and this unusual foot arrangement makes it even more confusing. They are wildly expressive, and their playfulness was obvious in the splatter and confusion of the tracks. One track was exceptionally sharp, and the webs between the toes were particularly distinct. The track was alive with detail, revealing the twisting, turning, and acceleration I had just seen, the dripping water carried from the channel, and the sand that had stuck to the feet and transferred into the track. . . .

It is thrilling to see an animal in action and immediately see its tracks, comparing the movements you just observed with the prints that were left. This is how the best trackers, the sand trackers, the Apaches of the Southwest and the Saan of Africa, gained their deep knowledge about the tiniest details of animal tracks and what they reveal. Thousands of years of close observation will add up!

Another favorite track was from a different water animal, the elusive muskrat. In several years of tracking club visits to the lagoons on Point Reyes, we have seen the rare muskrat only a few times, once busily harvesting cattail leaves next to the bridge, but we almost never find their tracks. Why not? Do they simply avoid coming on land here because of predation? We also never see the beaver lodge-type nests that they build in most other parts of the country. Here, they seem to prefer burrows with underwater entrances. In the muddy areas they inhabit, I was always on the lookout for them.

Finally, one warm evening, I found the perfect muskrat track, right at the edge of the water in damp sand at a "haul-out spot"—a gap in the cattail curtain allowing access to the shore. It was a track of the larger back foot, in its characteristic pigeon-toed position, and I could clearly see the web-like shelf of stiff hairs between the toes, along with the greatly undersized front foot track, which looks more like a typical rodent track, four toes splayed out in a star pattern, but larger than a mouse or a rat. It remains one of the great enigmatic mammal tracks, unique and rare in this area.

In a similar vein, I recently found beautiful tracks of a common coot in perfect soft fine sand near the shoreline of the lagoon. Coots spend most of their time paddling around in the shallows, dabbling like a mallard, busily devouring new water plant growth, and they don't come on land very often. It is worth trying to find a track because, though they are duck-like, they are more closely related to rails and don't have a truly webbed foot. Instead, they have evolved little flaps on the sides of their toes that flare out on the down stroke, creating something like a swimmer's fins or gloves. Only a good track on clean substrate will reveal this.

Otter webs, muskrat bristles, and coot flaps: three strikingly different morphological approaches to a common problem, the tracks revealing a hint of how diverse and responsive nature really is.

One of the most informative tracks of my life was back in New Jersey at a class with Tom Brown. He took us out to an area of very hard sandy soil where foxes emerge from the forest and cross to hunt in a meadow. Tom circled a blank spot in that hard, white, crystalline sand, in which he claimed was a fox track. He matter-of-factly told my group to start there and, when we could see that one, try to find the others.

For the next two hours I tried to see that track. I tried everything, ratcheting from wide-angle vision to tightly focused vision, laying my head right on the ground for extreme low-angle views, looking from different directions and different angles of light, breathing deeply, relaxing and surrendering, taking short walks and coming back to it. I did anything I could think of. I knew from many experiences that the ground does not reveal its secrets quickly. Sometimes it takes a while for the mind to adjust to the view. After a few minutes, tracks usually begin to pop into view. But this time, none of it worked. Within that small circle Tom had drawn, I saw nothing but sparkly white sand crystals on a flat surface. My head ached, and I felt exhausted.

Just as I was about to give up, as I let out a big breath and began to disengage, the track simply appeared, out of nowhere. I gave a startled yell. I could see the whole track, the little round toe pads and the heel pad, as if it had just been placed there. I can still see it: a nice, neat, round fox track, plain as day.

Then just as suddenly, it disappeared again. I stayed with it, elated with the strange feeling that some unfamiliar part of my brain was waking up. The track shimmered and fluttered in and out of my vision until I could finally hold it, and then I finally glimpsed a few more of the steps, tracks that had apparently been obvious to Tom, glowing with a light that is hard to explain in material terms. Physically, the track consisted of very small grains of sand pushed out of baseline. Baseline substrate in that location was a hard, flat surface that had undergone repeated cycles of damp and dry, rain and sun. It was packed and smooth. Those disturbed grains of white sand were hard to see, but once the eyes figured out what to look for, the patterns emerged, and they were in the shapes of toes.

It was only years later that I finally realized how Tom Brown had apparently seen the elusive fox track so easily. It was not some super-human ability, some extraordinary sense of vision, or some shamanistic tracker magic. He was simply deeply in tune with his land, with the Pine Barrens, where he had spent his life learning to track with his great mentor, Stalking Wolf. He knew how animal life was woven into this landscape, where the foxes slept and where they hunted. He could recognize their faint use trails where they went back and forth. He knew there had to be a track in that spot, and his well-trained eyes knew exactly what to look for.

There is something about tracking that beckons and teases, much like that fox track. It can draw us in to the power of the landscape. It can remind us of why we came here in the first place. Tracking can let us into the secret, hidden lives of the animals that surround us everywhere, and into their relationships with each other and with the landscape. It will draw us into the seasons and the weather, transforming us from mere nature tourists to becoming an integral part of the world, awakening our sense of oneness with the Earth and our link to our ancient ancestors who roamed these forests, fields, and beaches for thousands of years before us.

As eleven-year-olds, my brother and I were probing the tenuous body of real scout knowledge contained in the Boy Scout Manual. We were thirsty for any information about the Apaches and tracking that we could find. We knew instinctively that tracking held some keys to the magical kingdom of nature. We read about dragging a short log with nails set all around it, leaving drag tracks that a partner can try to follow. We tried it, late in summer vacation (the ground very dry), thinking it would be pretty easy. Instead, it left surprisingly few marks on the hard ground, and we were quickly discouraged and abandoned the project.

Oh, if only we had had a mentor, just one person who had a shred of information about this, who had the patience and persistence required, and who understood the outsized rewards to be reaped from the effort. If only there was one adult who could understand what we were trying to explore and who might have suggested we start practicing when the ground was softer in the winter. But no one had access to that world anymore. Without realizing it, we had just run into the Wall, the limit of our perceptual skill, and with no teachers and nothing more than a mere description of this old practice technique, we simply had nowhere to go when we got stumped.

It was only when I finally discovered Tom Brown's school and the Apache tracking skills that he had so fortunately inherited, that I found the door through that wall that had daunted me thirty years earlier. Finally, I began to discover the coyote's secret, the ability to silently absorb the subtle clues all around me and begin to merge into the spirit of nature.

Correspondingly, as I quickly learned, when we enter the landscape this way, it seems to welcome us, to include us in the amazing, sacred balance of life and death that nature has achieved. Approached through this door, this attitude, nature begins to unlock her secrets. The pieces of this complex puzzle begin to sort themselves out, and the way they fit makes complete sense. The landscape, the substrate, the weather, the time of day, the season of the year, the activities of the animals, where and how they step—it all fits together in a way that feels comfortable and natural to us, since we are part of the same processes that formed the evolution of life and its infinite expressions.

July 2008

Grass

I can't think of anything more exciting these days than watching the grass grow. I really mean that. It is even more exciting than watching paint dry! I've done that too: it's a lot more interesting than you might think to watch the solvents evaporate and the surface skim over. It is a beautiful organic process, like a pond freezing over. It's the same with grassy fields, only the process stretches out for months instead of minutes. It is key to the whole world of wildlife. It starts, just like paint, with a wet surface.

This year in particular, after three years of drought, the ground and the grass seeds were hungering deeply for a second rain in autumn, which is actually the one that typically germinates the seeds. That is the true start of spring in our Mediterranean climate, the first mass germination of new grasses and forbs, even though it is still only late fall. Things are a little upside down in the coastal climate.

But would the rains continue, would new grasses grow, or would they wither for lack of rain once again? This year, at last, it held. For weeks the new grass was barely visible on the hills, just a faint hint of green while the germinating plants concentrated on sending roots down into the damp soil, reaching for the increasing moisture as the length of days contradictorily shortened.

Before you knew it, we were past the winter solstice, and the days began to grow longer. Despite the dark clouds and colder temperatures, the grasses respond. It is all very slow at first, but once the roots are set, the growth surges. New roots and shoots take hold and advance in early January, in between cold spells, each time a warm rain sweeps through or a sunny break heats the earth in between cold storms.

As the season progresses and the rains keep coming, the past year's old dry grasses slowly break down, the new grasses flourish, and the hills suddenly turn bright green. Down at ground level, voles, the true base of the prey pyramid, begin a new cycle of expansion, fueled by the grass. Gophers get to work too, the softer ground and surge of plant growth reminding them that it's time to start re-building nests. All of this renewed rodent activity is great news for just about every predator in the neighborhood.

The fields and hillsides in the early part of this reawakening are a revelation. In addition to true grasses, the variety of plants is staggering. Of note in January and February are the blue-eyed grasses, related to irises, which are early to sprout and, with their bulb-root, capable of lasting through the dry season. These are the predominant early plants on poor draining soils, accompanied everywhere by dandelion, plantain, and sorrel. The corm plants survive cattle grazing well and supply dry-season food to gophers and voles. Late-season gopher and vole nests, often revealed by coyote or badger digs, are filled with the husks of their small bulbs, revealing the importance of this food source.

Deer, the true botanists in the herbivore world, are quick to find the most succulent and nutritious crops at any particular moment. Much can be learned from their choices, as they nibble-test their way across the landscape. Constant eaters, the deer are experts at finding fresh plant growth before the plants have been able to manifest their chemical protections in the form of bad tasting or toxic substances.

Of the up to eight hundred different species of plants a deer might eat during the course of a year, at any one moment they are probably feeding on only one or two dozen, the most nutritious species at that moment. In spring, their food variety is probably the greatest.

Each week is a new revelation, a new phase in the unfolding of the season of growth. The progress of spring shines in the neon flush across fields and forests. The earth warms and day-length increases, and we move from the Second Awakening into height of spring and a frenzy of growth and flowering, of bird song and birth. Migrations are underway. Creeks are running. Young mammals are born, ready to grow up and learn enough over summer to make it first through the dry season and then the first cold storms of their young lives next winter.

The grasses continue to grow through the spring into early summer when, much like the paint surface finally drying to the touch, the fields mature into grown plants with seed heads forming up. The green of spring fades into the golden hues of summer. Animals fade into the background too, no longer so concerned about seeing and being seen in courtship. Raising the kids and holding the home become the main concern, just as we humans move from spring into the summer and fall of our own lives.

June 2015

The Rabbits at Abbotts

Until about five years ago, black-tailed jackrabbits lived in high densities in the dunes and chaparral country both north and south of Abbotts Lagoon. At times, regular little highways of their trails snaked around the edges of the central basin, and I'd often flush one out of its little day bed (called a form) under a lupine bush. But the drought came, and with it the loss of their favorite sand dune succulents, and they simply disappeared. There has not been a track or scat to be found in this area for a few years now.

Soon after the jackrabbits disappeared, their primary predator, coyotes, quit hunting the basin and stopped scenting the territory with their scratch marks. Then, in a cascading sequence, several other animal patterns changed. Our cottontails, the little brush rabbits, often seen foraging on the new grass at the edges of trails, never far from thickets, began expanding their territories. In the rainy years before the big drought, the bunny population had gone through its own cycle of boom and bust. When once they literally lined the trails at dawn, a confluence of overpopulation and the sudden drought led to a fast decline.

Now, though, the disappearance of the coyotes and jackrabbits seemed to stimulate their recovery, and I began to find their tracks expanding into previously unoccupied areas. But gone were the jackrabbit highways and the scenes of their midnight gatherings. And gone as well were the beautiful curving trails of the coyotes and the tracks of their courting circles in mid-winter.

In this relative emptiness, a rare visitor made an appearance. A non-native red fox took up residence and began regularly patrolling the territory. Though I never saw it with my eyes, its tracks were unmistakable: right size, right shape, diagnostic details that can be made by no other animal. In particular, there is a V-shaped ridge on the heel pads of the front feet, known as the "chevron," that showed clearly in the proper substrates. Its travel patterns and gaits were unmistakable: entirely different than coyotes, who are the only possible animal its tracks could be mistaken for. It never dropped into the common "side-trot" gait of a coyote. Its foraging behavior reflected different goals. Instead of sweeping through the open areas in long undulating rhythms, hoping to flush out a rabbit the way coyotes do, the fox moved in erratic, fast-paced tours of the thickets, circling around them downwind, literally nosing around, assessing the mouse and brush rabbit presence. The appearance of the red fox accompanied the spread of the brush rabbit. It was a new equation: as the coyote is to the hare, so the fox is to the cottontail!

So go the population cycles in the natural world. But I missed those jackrabbits. With their unique features, the unusually long ears and long back legs, their strange lippity-lip rocking gait, sort of a combination of a lope and a hop, and their ability to explode into a high-speed escape, they are an iconic presence in our western landscape. How bemusing to see them gathered for their shindigs in the middle of the night, and how fascinating to unravel their tracks in the morning. With their blazing, elusive speed (thirty miles per hour with twenty-foot leaps) and their excellent hearing, they don't seem very worried about predators, not even the coyote. And while the brush rabbit thinks in terms of square feet, the jackrabbit thinks in terms of miles. A courting chase between amorous jackrabbits can cover several miles over the course of a night. It is an exciting, high-presence animal.

When I drive by one of their get-togethers in the fields near my home late at night or just before dawn, I stop the car and watch for a while, leaving the headlights on. They pay no attention to the car and the lights. It looks like they are going through a choreographed, almost hypnotic dance performance. One moves a few steps, stops, and stands up on its hind legs. Then another moves a few steps and stops. There may be several of them involved in these rituals. One at a time they move around, stop, and sit upright, holding their long ears still and erect, then drop down, take a few more steps and stop again.

Maybe it's the white eye rings around their large eyes, as if wearing glasses, that gives them a professorial, almost intellectual look, or maybe it's their insistence that the party not be interrupted, the almost zombie-like state they are in. But there is something unworldly about them. Native peoples sensed this, revering them as wise tricksters and shape shifters. I see this in their trails. With their long back legs, their bounding gait stretches out when they move fast, and their trail can easily be mistaken for a coyote gallop. How silly it can make a tracker feel to be fooled that way!

During the agricultural takeover of the American West in the late 1800s and the tragic effort to kill virtually all wildlife that posed a threat to crops and herds, jackrabbits were shot, poisoned, and clubbed by the millions in large-scale hunting drives. Given the estimates that thirty jackrabbits can eat as much grass as one cow, the competitive threat for scarce resources is understandable. They were largely extirpated in the northwest wheat country, but like their coyote adversary, they survived the onslaught, and we are lucky they did, though their former abundance is greatly reduced.

So yes, I missed them out on the coast. Like bobcats, their presence felt somehow reassuring. Yet recently, six or eight years after the drought and their decline, and just as the verbena, their favorite succulent, has recovered in the normal rainfall of the last two years, I have begun finding evidence of their return. Remarkably, they have re-established the same old trail systems and gathering locations. On one recent morning, I found evidence of one of the "boxing matches," a courting behavior they are famous for, which gave rise to the phrase "mad as a March hare." The signs of male-to-male combat were plain to see: heavy scratches and long, sharp digs made by the hares' rear feet when they rose up facing each other to fight in sort of a hand-to-hand combat, while the females crouched around the edges, watching and choosing.

Along with the return of the jackrabbits, the coyotes reappeared as well, and that red fox disappeared as mysteriously as it arrived, either killed or pushed out. The coyotes took up residence, established a den, and raised a litter this summer. I see the tracks and trails of the kids running around now—not quite as purposeful as the adults, but beginning to fall into the same patterns as they grow up and learn to hunt. The resident bobcat in the thicket moved out for the summer, its favored dens and day-beds too close to the coyotes for comfort, and she raised her own kids farther back in the brush, where voles, gophers, and quail are plentiful in the open chaparral. But now, as we move into fall and the young coyotes disperse, I'm beginning to see her tracks returning to the old routines. The cycles circle around once more.

August 2017

The World of Bird Tracks

When I first began learning how to track animals, the thought of tracking birds seemed a little crazy—how can you track a bird through the air? But once I started studying bird tracks, I realized that most of them spend a substantial amount of time on the ground and leave tracks virtually everywhere. Just like mammals, each species has a unique foot shape, a unique habitat and foraging style, and unique signs of its activities.

Many birders focus primarily on identifying a bird, perhaps observing a little of its behavior, and, satisfied, move on to the next one, quickly bored with common species. Birds are great fun to identify, with their beautiful, varied plumage, and highly specialized adaptations to every habitat, but for a tracker, the "life list" is unimportant and rare sightings are not particularly valuable. Once we begin to understand how much information about the local birds and their activities can be found throughout the landscape, and how much it can tell us about the inter-relationships between the landscape and all of the animals in it, the lowly "little brown bird" becomes as important a source of the information we are after as a rare exotic. It is the story of the land, of nature in all its wonderfully complex radiance we are after. This is the call we hear.

As with mammals, the landscape plays the birds like musical instruments, conducting them in a grand performance, every note connected to the whole symphony of life. It all fits. If we take the time to look, we find a detailed record of these lives in their tracks and signs. While the movements, sounds and rhythms of their calls tell the current story of the landscape, the tracks and signs tell a story of the past few hours, days and weeks. It is not difficult to learn to read bird tracks. Like any language, it just takes a little getting used to. With their infinite variations, bird feet, like all aspects of avian morphology, are minutely adapted to each species' niche in world. It all makes sense in nature. Everything is designed for a specific purpose. The joy in tracking is that when we begin to see the connections between design and purpose, we see a little deeper into the lives of the familiar birds around us.

There are four basic bird foot shapes, four categories of bird tracks: classic, game bird, webbed foot, and "zygodactyl."

The classic bird track has one long back toe (the hallux) and three toes forward, the equivalent of our thumb and first three fingers. Birds with this foot tend to be perching birds like warblers, sparrows, and thrushes, as well as jays, blackbirds, herons, and hawks. With the long back toe and the large toe pads, they can firmly grip round branches.

Game birds like quail, turkeys, and plovers, who live and feed mostly on the ground and do not perch by gripping small branches, have a much smaller back toe and heavy toe pads, leaving a knobby three-toed track.

The swimming birds—such as ducks, geese, and gulls—have three webbed front toes and a reduced back toe, except in the case of the pelican and cormorant, whose webs (called totipalmate) connect all four toes.

Finally, there is the specialized zygodactyl foot, with two toes forward and two toes back, found on owls, woodpeckers, and osprey. On these birds, the outer front toe, the equivalent of our ring finger, has rotated around to the back for different gripping purposes.

Each of these foot forms is connected with a particular part of the landscape, and the landscape can indicate what birds will be present, at what time of year, and where their tracks and signs are likely to be found. Of course, the same goes for mammals and any other form of life. A track is not random. Each track is deeply connected to the whole web of life, to nature in all her complexity.

Each species of bird, like mammals, has a typical way of moving on the ground, their baseline gait. It is, of course, "bi-pedal," like humans. Bird gaits range from walking to running and from hopping to skipping. The ground foragers and the waders, such as quail, ravens, gulls, and herons, tend to walk. Sparrows, juncos, and jays tend to hop or skip. Specialized feeders such as sanderlings, who feed at surf lines, or robins working a forest floor for worms, tend to run.

The patterns of deviation from these baseline gaits are one of the ways that tracks begin to speak, telling us how the birds behaved, what they noticed, and how they felt. The tracks begin to tell a story of how the birds reacted to events around them, what those events might have been, and even what we might expect now.

Expressive as tracks can be, the world of bird sign is even more revealing. Cough pellets, common in scavengers and predators, give insight into diet, habits, and favored perching locations. Bone fragments and hair or feather in the pellets reveal the types of prey available and the range of the hunter. Droppings, when inspected closely, provide clues to the identification, range, diet, and ecology of the bird in question. Insect parts, seeds, berries, and plant fibers can often be identified, offering information about bird territories.

Feeding signs are revealing because each bird leaves a characteristic signature of its presence. For example, some perching birds, particularly finches, feed at sources, leaving seed chaff and fluff at dismantled thistle heads, while others, such as chickadees and titmouses, carry food away to perches where the chaff and debris accumulates. Feeding on fruits will leave distinctive pecking patterns. Bud-feeding on shrubs can leave a burnt appearance at branch tips.

Every aspect of the bird's morphology reveals the great length of time they've been evolving, possibly hundreds of millions of years, and every part of a bird, from beak and wing to feather and foot, is uniquely designed for effectiveness in a precise niche. Sign tracking leads one right into the heart of what makes each species unique.

At Limantour Beach, the larger long-legged godwits and dowitchers wade in deeper waters, sandpipers forage in shallower waters, sanderlings run up and down in the wave-wash zone, and plovers hunt in higher, drier areas. But even within each of these gradients, bird species are further refined by the size of food they seek, their beaks carefully designed for specific prey or seed. Each of these shorebirds leaves a characteristic pattern of bill probes and track doodles, which in turn reveal underlying food sources.

In the oak-lands, acorns are a rich source of information. Every animal has developed its own method of accessing the nutritious nut inside. Acorn woodpeckers carry the acorns to ancient granary trees, drilling holes by the thousands, carefully fitting one acorn into each hole. They come back later to drill into the end to eat either the nut-meat, or later in the year, the weevils in it, which provide more protein during the nesting season. Crows and jays, on the other hand, often carry acorns and other scavengings to a perch, known as an anvil, and hold them down with one foot while breaking them open with their beaks (the sound loud like a woodpecker, but more erratic), leaving chaff accumulations with jagged shell edges below the perch.

Each of the other species of woodpecker in the forest is adapted to specific insect prey and has a specific drumming rhythm and quality of sound. The smaller woodpeckers, such as the downy woodpecker, will probe living trees with a faster and sharper "ratatat" drumming sound than the large pileated woodpeckers, who will often excavate for carpenter ants in deadwood with a slower, softer "thunk, thunk" sound, leaving huge excavations known as woodpecker sculptures.

Feathers and their scatter patterns around kill sites can reveal who the primary predators are. Peregrines commonly eat their avian prey near shorelines and other edges, often leaving a fully connected set of wing bones stripped of meat down to the primary feathers, with the plucked body feathers scattered around in a small "fairy" circle. There will be no large crushed or severed bones, only a broken breast keel with triangular cutouts from their bills. Coyotes and bobcats, on the other hand, will break and crush wing bones and leave the plucked feathers in a wider scattering.

This is just a glimpse of the possibilities in bird tracking. Like all tracking, each insight leading to more insights as one realization after another dawns on us, and the often-invisible aspects of bird life and their intricate relationships with the plants and animals around them become more and more apparent.

October 2011

A Simple Walk

A simple two-hour tracking walk through any particular landscape can turn up an astounding amount of information about what is going on just under the surface. It is always exciting to enter the natural world through this door and watch what happens.

Let's do it! Let's go take a walk along a trail through chaparral-covered hills near the coast.

First, even before we arrive, let's connect with the location, noting the time of day, the season, and current conditions. It is eight in the morning on a calm and clear summer day. Remember recent weather patterns: the wind and rain, the warm and cold cycles. It has been damp and foggy, but pleasant, with a good break from the cyclical coastal winds. The moon has been waning, and therefore setting early, meaning that the early hours before dawn were very dark. We are letting our minds reach forward and flow into the landscape, letting our inner thought-tracks subside and our senses wake up.

Notice the wind: blowing lightly from the north, with a subdued hush. Feel the sun on your skin, warming steadily, and feel the moisture in the air, the morning still young. Take a few slow steps, the beginning of a shift. Walk very slowly for a few moments, coordinating your breath with your steps. Inhale deeply and release into a long easy exhale, letting your whole body relax. Look up in a broad view of the landscape, taking it all in, widening your view as much as possible, seeing the play of light and color and the patterns of movement, holding this for a moment. Let it expand, listening to the symphony of the whole landscape. We are re-animating the world, letting it come to life around us, heightening our senses and our awareness. Bird calls are surprisingly varied. Far in the background, the distant surf steadily drones, easily forgotten but ever-present.

Now we can begin tracking. The whole landscape, in its wild profusion, has a story to tell. Many questions quickly come to mind. Who is likely to be out here? Where are the comfort zones? Where is the shelter? Where is the food? Where is the water? Where are the vantage points? Where are the hideouts and deepest thickets? Where do I feel drawn right now? And of course: where is the good track substrate, the dust, the mud, or the sand? All it takes is one partial track, embedded in its context, to tell a whole story.

Keep listening. What do the patterns of the birdcalls tell us? Who else is calling? How does the wind sound, and where are its notes coming from? How do our footsteps and voices sound?

Smells, too: where has this breeze been, and what is its story? What are the smells right around us? Awareness and curiosity soon turn to amazement and wonder as the earth comes alive and begins to speak.

We step down the trail. The sparrow and quail have already sent out an alarm and are busily repositioning themselves. Sentinels have perched in the tops of the ripening coyote brush, and quail are abandoning their feeding activities. One female dashes across the gravelly trail, and we go up to inspect. Not quite attuned yet, we are surprised that there are no tracks. How could that be? We just saw the bird run across. It's not great substrate, but we should be seeing something.

We stop and, together, take another breath and relax. Sure enough, what had first appeared to be random marks begin to assemble. Right there in front of me, one track after another comes into focus. The toes appear, then the knuckle bumps and the toenails. Then the pressure releases reveal themselves, the tiny ridges and blowouts reporting the haste and direction shifts of the startled bird as it ran. We begin to see the layers of older tracks, the feeding patterns, the history of this spot. Mixed in are a few narrow and delicate sparrow tracks, in paired hop patterns, and below all that, insect and worm trails cover the ground.

So here, at the first opportunity, our eyes are embracing this story written on the earth. Our minds are built to search for these patterns and make sense of them, but we have to give ourselves time to let our minds do their work. It is odd how little respect we give our minds, how we expect them to see and absorb everything at once. Our brain needs time, a little kindness and patience, to work properly and do its job. It is astounding to watch details appear, like lights coming on, as our perceptual apparatus processes the huge amount of information we are taking in.

We continue scanning the ground, and our next glance lands on little hollows in fine sandy soil nearby, and we realize that these aren't random surface contours; they are the dust baths the quail were using in the early sun. Quickly coming into focus, with this realization, are the subtle swirl marks of their fluttering wing and tail feathers around the edges of the small depressions. Indeed, now that we are alert, we see a few small coverlet feathers that lie around the margins of the depressions, brown feathers with the tan edgings typical of quail.

Next to them is a small black-and-white bird scat just below a projecting branch. The dark part is composed of shiny pieces of insect carapace, perhaps from a phoebe who had been using the branch as a hunting perch, swooping out to catch insects rising into the warming air.

Looking closer, we notice a small round passage hole, about four inches in diameter, through the curtain of grasses at the trail-edge and the little furry-footed scoot-outs of a small brush rabbit as it leapt back into cover just before we arrived. Sure enough, there is the fresh mown look of the tender grasses it had been browsing, with a couple of old scat pellets attesting to its regular presence. I crouch down and peer through the rabbit run. As my eyes adjust, I'm startled to see that, Alice in Wonderland-like, the little rabbit is crouched behind a lupine stem just a foot or two away; it stares back at me, trembling slightly, its bright eye shining, hoping it is well hidden, waiting for me to pass so it can resume its meal. Of course, I ease back in a gesture of respect.

Just a bit further along the edge of the trail, where a grassy field comes close, is a large, airy, twisted and folded mammal scat, composed of fine, short brown fur. A look out over the field reveals, not surprisingly, numerous gopher mounds, and indeed, a few large, industrious digs. This coyote scat marks a good spot for hunting one of its favorite prey this year. A closer look at the scat is rewarded: a beautiful lower jawbone with long sharp, orange-tinted incisors emerges, with the extra flange on the side and the molar pattern identifying it as gopher. Tracking will turn you into an osteologist! Glancing along the trail, we notice two or three medium-sized partial tracks on the edge, a little weathered and disturbed, but still holding the internal X-pattern with the high dome in the middle; it can be nothing other than a coyote track, corroborating the scat identification.

Quickly, two hours have passed and we've only moved a hundred yards down the trail. Our schedule seems less important than before, and the call to stay out and pull back the layers of this world is irresistible. Fitness walking will have to fit in another time. This is an entirely different kind of exercise, a different journey. It can be dangerous to start paying attention. We run the risk of feeling a new level of aliveness in ourselves and a new depth of connection and camaraderie with nature itself, a sense of fitting in and belonging. It calls and activates an insidious sense of rebellion that rises from our core. We are hearing the call of our wild, and the urge to reprioritize some of our goals and commitments.

Yes! Let's miss that appointment, postpone that chore, make that phone call later. With another hour or two, right now, having already immersed ourselves, we might make it down the trail another hundred yards and deep into the fire of life and nature in all its radiance.

September 2011

Spring: The Second Awakening—March

Spring is always a favorite season as we emerge from the depths of the cold nights and short days of winter. Who is not gladdened by this season, by the explosive growth and activity in nature, by the blossoming of our trees and flowering of our meadows and hillsides? Who does not find joy in the return of migrating birds and the busy nesting season with its musical calls and songs? Who does not love gamboling in the lengthening and warming days, across the picture-book landscape, with its brilliant green slopes, blue skies, scattered clouds, and soft, warm soils?

It is good to remember, though, that here in our coastal Mediterranean climate, spring is actually the second awakening, a re-awakening if you will. The longest slumber in our region is in the late summer and fall (not winter) when the creeks have run dry and rain is a distant memory, when the hills have turned brown, food supplies have dwindled and prey populations decline.

Usually reliable, the first rains arrive in late September and October, increase in November and become earnest in December. The early rains set off an explosion of plant growth and animal activity as everyone gets busy preparing for the long nights and cold days of the winter slump.

That was the First Awakening.

Late December and January bring freezing nights and mornings. A long pause ensues. The whole plant world more or less shuts down, and animals, from insects to mammals, hunker down to wait it out. Some, such as our skunks, will dip into quasi-hibernation in the coldest weeks. Others continue to prowl, just getting by, simply trying to stay dry and fed enough to make it through.

But suddenly, it seems, March arrives. The days grow noticeably longer, temperatures begin to rise, and the storms ease into pleasant showers. It goes by fast, this transition time. The whole of nature responds, as if it was waiting for a signal. For the last two months it was as if the Creator were winding up a spring, ready to let it go when the time was right. . . .

This is the Second Awakening!

Nature explodes into action. Now it is a race to grow faster, to feed heavier, to burst into flower, to build nests and dens and burrows, to give birth and launch the kids. Food is abundant at all levels and everyone is fattening up, establishing new boundaries, and living in the gladness of the land.

A walk in mid-March, in an area with good sandy or muddy substrate, will reveal endless signs of this explosive reawakening. Sparrows are out in force: some year-round residents, some migrators. White crowns are active in the chaparral, obvious at the tops of the tallest shrubs, singing their hearts out, defining their new territories, sorting out mates. Along the sides of trails, trident-shaped sparrow tracks may cover the ground, some in hops, some in skips. Around marshy areas, blackbirds spend more time foraging on the ground, leaving their amusing stitched track patterns, their heads bobbing forward and back with each step.

Raptors, from kestrels to harriers, are sweeping through, eyeing the growing insect and rodent populations. Coots are still gathering near shorelines in small flotillas. Marsh wrens are chattering noisily in the cattails, beginning to build their new basket nests. They've got to be one of the noisiest birds in nature, incessantly calling back and forth, safe in the cattail stalks, just beyond the shorelines. Black phoebes, like all flycatchers, are very active, flitting out from their perches to make mid-air snatches in the growing clouds of gnats and other insects. Swallows are sweeping back and forth over the waterways.

Ravens, still in large groups, are pairing up with their mates, thinking about stick gathering and nest building. I often refer to April as "stick season" because crows and ravens can so often be seen carrying sticks in their bills, making beelines to their nest sites, some new, some ancestral. How handy of nature to have wind-pruned the trees over the last couple of months, leaving such a bounty of construction materials lying on the ground just in time for the Second Awakening.

Brush rabbits line the trails at dawn, and the brambly thickets are pierced with their little escape tunnels. In ungrazed sections of meadows and fields, where last year's old grasses still provide cover, the newly increasing population of field voles is busy once again, creating their telltale mazes of half-tunnels through the new-growing grasses around the perimeters of the lupines. In sand dunes, there is a new burst of mouse activity, covering the ground with nightly track speckles amongst the grasses and shrubs as they work to replenish food caches exhausted during the winter storms.

Raccoons are busy again too, their double track patterns creating obvious trails from brushy hideouts to water edges where they love to forage for the shoreline crustaceans and the much-treasured, soon-abundant, carelessly placed bird nests where they seek eggs. Skunks are wandering about in their erratic foraging routes, thoroughly exploring every brushy edge, finding insect concentrations, leaving the scattered patterns of their little conical digs.

Frogs also are out and about. With the warming weather, there is a burst of dispersal journeys as they head to higher land or from one water body to another, sometimes leaving shockingly long, relentlessly steady hopping trails across open expanses. Along with the frogs, more snakes are making crossings to favored habitat, leaving beautiful, undulating swirls in substrates soft enough to record their passing.

Much of this activity is due to the sudden increase in insect activity. The ant-headed beetle can be amazingly active and abundant, and will travel in extremely long foraging routes—hundreds of feet at times, hunting ground-nesting wasp larvae and other buried prey, leaving a very characteristic track, little hockey-stick shaped marks on either side of a deep body drag. Millipedes are also out in sudden abundance, circling around and around in their foraging routes, while small subsurface burrowing beetles, shaped like miniature Volkswagens, with a hard, smooth carapace, leave endless squiggling trails in loose sands. Even the great horned owls are profiting from the insect bloom, leaving long zig-zagging trails of their unique K-shaped tracks across open sands as they walk or run from one beetle sighting to another.

Meanwhile, the coyotes have paired up after courting during the winter and are running together, leaving their beautifully choreographed side trots and lopes. Sometimes, especially after a rain, they will be hurrying through their territories, re-marking their scent posts and leaving vigorous scrapes and scratches on the ground, where they are transferring their signature scents from the glands between their toes on to the ground surface. With the increase in rodent and bird prey, our bobcats are also relaxing a little, roaming a little farther, apparently glad to break up their normal routines.

Badgers are on the move, roaming from one rich gopher zone to another, circling (in the time-honored predator tradition) a territory that is large enough to let prey populations recover before they return. Their trails can sometimes be followed as they inspect old burrows and dig zones, probing the ground for fresh scent, listening deeply for sounds of activity.

All this time, since the flurry of rutting season during the First Awakening, deer have been quietly hanging back, rebuilding their reserves, separated into "milk groups" of related females growing heavy with pregnancy, while the males have formed little bachelor groups, the original fraternal orders, resting and fattening after the rigors of the rut, and now ready to begin the cycle all over again, little buds of antler tips already beginning to form. Both the bucks and the does are leaving very obvious trails back and forth across open areas in their relentless wide-spread browsing habit, settling in here and there for an hour or two of napping and digesting, before continuing on, expertly selecting the most nutritious plants to nibble.

Before long, this springtime exuberance begins to ease into the long fullness of summer. There will be a day when the forests and thickets seem suddenly quiet again, when we might be inclined to wonder where everyone went, as the business of raising the new generation becomes the focus, and the animal world becomes a little more cautious and furtive. But for now, each day is a new adventure and the urge to get out into the sparkling mornings and warm afternoons is impossible to resist.

June 2015

The Ground We Stand On

Tracking is really the study of life in the dynamic, ongoing present. But a study of animals and plants inevitably involves a study of the landscape. This in turn leads to the geology of the underlying land, since geological history determines the evolution of life forms. The geology in West Marin is some of the most complex in the world. We can find rock that is four hundred million years old alongside major landscape features formed in just the last few thousand years.

The fields at the foot of Tomales Bay might well be the most complex and dynamic location in the Bay Area. A walk out there is a walk through time and space. Near the old railway levee are still-exposed cuts in the hillside from the narrow-gauge railroad construction in the late 1800s, revealing a wide variety of rock types and shapes. This ground is a complex mixture of gravel, rock, and mud: the famous Franciscan Mélange, perhaps five to ten thousand feet deep, containing hard, shiny chunks of red chert alongside hard basalt, river-rounded sandstone, broken-up shale, bits of granite, and occasional volcanic rocks.

The chert has come from the furthest reaches of ocean floor, at the Pacific spreading center, two or three thousand miles away. This rock is composed of microscopic radiolarian shells, which accumulated on the sea crust for over one hundred and fifty million years. Driven along on the basaltic ocean crust in its westward tectonic journey, it transformed into this hard chert, as it moved slowly toward its rendez-vous with the coast and the lighter continental plate. There, it was partially scraped off at the edge of the subduction zone as the basaltic crust dove under the continental plate.

At the same time, the scraper edge of the continental plate is composed of ancient sedimentary rocks, the remnants of former mountain ranges. They eroded into shallow seas, hardened, lifted, broke up, washed down again, and fell into the subducting trench to be churned, compacted, transformed again, and spit back out as our common outcrop rock, the greywacke, and many other forms of coastal sandstones and shales.

The greywacke formed when offshore earthquakes caused massive undersea landslides, the sedimentary sandstone seabed consolidating in massive compacted formations at the bottom of deep erosional trenches, only to be then sucked into the subduction trench between the two colliding tectonic plates, transformed into a harder rock. Later faulting broke these formations up and brought them to the surface to mix into the rest of the land sediments. It has been estimated that enough material washed into the sea from the land, and down into the heat of the subduction trench, to create enough greywacke to cover California with a layer over 10,000 feet thick! This is the amount of erosion that can take place over hundreds of millions of years.

The rounded river rocks in our Franciscan Mélange are remnants of ancient rivers that shifted, changed, eroded, and washed out over great spans of time. The volcanic fragments are from the arcs of vol-canos that rose and spouted behind the subduction zone, where the heat of the ongoing collision melted the basement rock and sent it to the surface.

Finally, the basalts and serpentine that underlie the chert layers, which are also mixed into the mélange, were the actual melted mantle rock that was bubbling up and spreading at the deep mid-ocean ridge where the seafloor spreads, the generator of the whole system.

As if this dynamic mixture weren't enough, it is only a part of the puzzle. Here at the edge of the San Andreas Fault, right across Tomales Bay, the massive Inverness Ridge is chugging northward like a slow-moving train, blocking this part of the coastline from the ocean, influencing weather, vegetation, and landscapes.

The Inverness Ridge, and Point Reyes Peninsula as a whole, is the southern tip of the granitic batholith that bubbled up to form the Sierra Nevada Mountains around one hundred million years ago. Sliced off by faulting, it is currently traveling up the coast, squeezed by pressure between the Pacific Plate and the North American Plate. On its journey, it accumulated several pulses of sedimentary rocks that make up the cliffs of Drakes Bay and the broad basin between Inverness Ridge and the outlying cliffs of Point Reyes itself. But some of the overlying rocks on the point are older than the granite batholith itself.

At the northern edge of this traveling block are remnants of even older sedimentary rocks that at one time lay above the granite, a roof that was pushed up by the rising granitic pluton. The heat and pressure of the rising molten granite transformed those original sedimentary rocks into some of the hardest and most beautiful rocks on the peninsula: gneiss. It is impossible to tell how old some of the base layers of sediment are, but they are at least three hundred to four hundred million years old, possibly the remnants of two or more mountain-building orogenies—about when life was first emerging from the sea and beginning to colonize the land! The source rock is very similar to rock in the Mojave Desert in southeast California.

Drakes Estero was hollowed out by rainfall erosion, when the sea level was four hundred feet lower than it is now, during the last glacial epochs twenty thousand years ago. Like San Francisco Bay—where the Golden Gate was once a massive waterfall—the estero is a drowned river valley.

The San Andreas is not the only fault line in the Bay Area. There are several of them in a zone nearly one hundred miles wide, stretching inland to Sacramento. With all this slip and thrust faulting, all this slicing, dicing, and folding of the coastal lands for hundreds of millions of years, the ground is now a mishmash of rock types and ages.

So this is our story: ocean floors spreading and traveling thousands of miles, coastlines grinding away, sea bottoms diving deeply under continental crust to re-melt and push upward again, mountain ranges that rise and fall over one- to two-hundred-million-year cycles.

There is more. The tectonic plates of the earth's surface are restless. After pushing directly against the continent for hundreds of millions of years, the Pacific Plate changed direction and began heading northward, creating the coastal faulting systems. But more recently, perhaps only five to ten million years ago, it shifted yet again and began pushing at an angle against the continent, causing the folding that created the characteristic rolling shapes of our coastal hills. This rumpling made new erosional patterns that formed our rounded valleys and left the hard greywacke outcrops exposed on the hillsides, bobbing in the surface of the mélange like raisins in pudding.

It is startling to walk across these landscapes and realize how dynamic and changing it all is. The earth is not nearly as stable as it looks from the perspectives of a few human lifetimes, or even human history.

Each of us is much the same as this landscape. We are all separate entities, whole humans, but we are made up of a genetic history older than the mixture of rocks on Railroad Point—as old as life itself. We contain within us material from vast tectonic journeys, epochs of migrations, and ancient cultural histories. In each of our present lives, we have picked up various portions of the world's politics, philosophies, and cultural values, along with influences from all the individuals and communities we have spent time with. We are all a Franciscan Mélange, an underlying mix that has been sliced, stirred, and faulted. We are literally part of the ground we stand on.

August 2015

Stripping Down

This question comes up occasionally: "What kind of gear or equipment do I need to go tracking?" I have guidebooks that go into this subject at great length. One, by a very knowledgeable New England tracker, provides a list that includes an internal frame pack, five-inch knife, disposable gloves, heat packets, duct tape, waterless disinfectant, binoculars, camera, headlamp with spotlight intensity, electronic heat detector, pen-type microscope, casting kit with spray wax, bowls, dishes, paper towels, compass, backup compass, maps, twelve-channel GPS, high-ankle waterproof lace-to-toe boots, and extra socks.

I have a somewhat different view.

I think we can become better trackers, and learn more about the world we inhabit, in inverse proportion to how much baggage and equipment, both external and internal, we drag along.

To me, the most important piece of equipment we can bring when we head out into the landscape is our awareness. No kit to bring will provide this. It is internal. We come automatically equipped with it, but we are charged with the responsibility of learning how to use it. External equipment can easily get in the way. All it really takes to be a tracker is the willingness to walk out into the world without haste or destination. Our bodies and minds can take care of the rest. But this is not a simple task.

Once we have gotten ourselves outdoors, anywhere from the wooded trails to the windy beaches, or simply into our own backyards, the first piece of gear to pull out of our internal kit is a long, deep breath, slowly drawn in and slowly released as it triggers us to quiet our mental dialogue and tune into the world around us. Sounds, smells, colors, and visual details intensify as we begin to re-enter the actual present moment. This is the state in which we start to see and connect all the little bits of information around us as we literally begin to perceive a world that had previously been invisible. No heat detector, for example, is required to determine which tracks are freshest once we have learned to actually see.

The human body is remarkably resilient, with millions of years of evolutionary development in its ability to respond and adapt to the conditions of the outdoors. So the second-most important piece of equipment to bring along is a willingness to experience temporary discomfort and allow our body to respond. It will. If we learn not to resist, the fog and cold, or the sun and heat, become allies instead of adversaries. My teacher once told a great story about a moment after he and his friend had been following their Apache mentor, Stalking Wolf, in the woods for a few years, through summer heat waves and winter snow storms, sleeping in survival shelters and living close to the land. They noticed that Stalking Wolf never seemed bothered by the weather. Finally, they asked him why he never minded the incredible heat or cold that they suffered. He answered simply: "Because they are real." Instead of resisting the earth, he embraced it. He understood that suffering was only in the mind.

We usually walk through the world with thick layers of insulation. We are taught, from our very beginnings, by our "civilized" culture, to be wary of the earth, to get as far from it as possible, even to fear or hate it. We encase ourselves in heavy shoes, heavy coats, and heavy thoughts. We hide in our minds and learn to wear a public mask that always expresses that we are *just fine*. We insulate and isolate ourselves in the name of safety and comfort and the fervent hope that we will be liked and accepted by our fellow humans. Of course, it doesn't work, because we lose our authenticity and become strangers to our own selves.

So I say, leave the equipment behind. Keep taking things off! Let your body discover how to draw upon its inner reserves. Put the cold outside of yourself where it actually is. Feel the heat and flow with it. Experience the sun and the wind. Try taking less every time you go out. Less food, less water, less stuff, less fear. Relax instead. It is amazing how little you actually need. You will learn to know your own self, to listen to your body and respect your natural strengths.

I say: bare your soles! Feel the earth under your feet. Walk free for a while. Jump in a lake! Roll in the mud! Liberate yourself.

In this state, you can truly become a tracker. It will help you understand how nature is organized, why the plants and animals chose their particular patterns, where animals are likely to be. Plants and animals in turn will respond differently to you. And the tracks you find will mean more, because you are becoming a part of them, a real local, instead of an alien dropped from some other planet, encased in a psychological spacesuit and layers of insulation.

Turn into the wind. Imagine you are a coyote, sniffing deeply into that breeze, drinking in the wealth of smells. Feel the breeze. Feel the wild howl of joy welling up from within you, the primal joy, the urge to run! Get naked! Just for the heck of it.

August 2011

Sacred Questions

Tracking is a constant learning process, an accumulation of observations that expands our ability to interpret the signs of animal activity. From this well of experience, we learn to quickly construct, from tiny details, an accurate picture of current activity in any particular landscape. Nevertheless, in nature we are constantly confronted with mysteries that challenge our understanding. In fact, the more we learn to observe, the more questions will arise to confound us.

In tracker jargon, these are called "sacred questions," meaning simply that we hold them gently without demanding immediate answers. We observe the mystery and file the question away in our minds. Held that way, in a semi-unconscious state but with a little light left blinking, so to speak, we accumulate more information until some pertinent key brings the answer. Sometimes this will happen in minutes or hours. Sometimes it takes years for a critical piece of information, or a chance observation, to fall into place in a moment of sudden realization.

The answer might come from a simple observation, something never noticed before, a passage in a book previously glossed over, or a chance remark in a conversation. Sometimes it is just a matter of putting two and two together in one's own mind. The "sacred" part is the matter of honoring the question but letting it stand unanswered, simply filing it away and holding it until that "ah-ha" moment arrives and the picture comes into focus. The sacredness lies in how fruitful such questions can be in leading us to into the mysteries of nature.

I vividly remember a morning over ten years ago, when I was out tracking with a group in some coastal hills. It was late spring. We stopped along an old ranch road where runoff from a recent rain had been backing up in mud-edged pools. Mud being great track substrate, we immediately fanned out to take a look. The wet edges of the mud were covered with tiny tracks! Mice? Sparrows? The location, an open field, didn't make sense for either of these possibilities. The details refused to fall into place. Perplexed, we filed it away as a sacred question and moved on.

We continued down the lane and, a mile or so from those puddles, came to an old barn, wide open and unused for many years. It was a treasure trove of dusty rodent tracks, lizard and toad scat, owls and their cough pellets, and dozens of barn swallows swooping around in the eaves, busily building their mud-dab nests, flying off and coming back.

As the day came to a close and we headed home, we found ourselves walking by the mud puddles again. As the question about the mysterious mud tracks pulled at the back of my mind, a couple of barn swallows pecked at the edges of the mud. *Bingo.* Suddenly it all fell into place. This was the source of the material for their building projects back at the barn, mud of perfect consistency, well worth the long flight back to the best nest location. They were scooping up bills-full and flying it back, leaving the puddles fringed with little v-shaped gouges: the tracks we couldn't identify. It had never occurred to me that swallows would fly that far for proper mud. It helped me learn to think like a bird, to view the earth through the advantage of wings.

One surprising question arose just outside my house. As I found myself noticing more of what was around me, I slowly became aware of a growing number of big earth domes scattered across the fields, some up to eighteen inches tall and thirty-six inches in diameter. Had they always been there, and I just hadn't noticed? Or had more of them appeared in the last three or four wet winters, when that ground becomes saturated and the water table is only inches below the surface of the ground?

Were they giant gopher mounds? Why so unusually large? What else could they be? Badger throw-mounds? There certainly were not any holes of corresponding size dug anywhere near them, although as I became more curious, I began to notice that some of them were recently dug into by coyotes, and there were remnant wads of dried grasses—rodent nest materials—mixed into the throw mounds.

Finally, curiosity drove me to take a shovel out there to see what was in a dome, and voila! There was a large gopher nest inside, stuffed with dried grass, with well-used runs going down in two directions. What a relief to finally verify my hunches. I may even be witnessing a process of evolution, as this strategy seems to work in terms of survivability; the mounds are proliferating. This local gopher population may be learning a new skill, or perhaps they are employing an old strategy in response to new conditions. Animals and plants have evolved over enormous lengths of time. What exists now is what worked over time and was able to survive through wildly changing environmental conditions and climatic cycles. Perhaps somewhere in the genetic memory of the gophers is this response to heavy rain cycles and saturated ground.

Here was an amazingly delicate and subtle balance of survival on the edges. These domes put the nests above the water table, making survival and successful reproduction possible, yet exposing the nest to easier digging and predation by coyote or badger. It may be that the high clay content of this particular soil, hardening the dome once it settles and dries out, is the critical edge that gives the gophers time to give birth, raise the young, and get them to safer underground tunnels.

The first recorded sighting of a black bear on the Point Reyes Peninsula in one hundred years offered a sacred question that took many weeks to address. I was called out to look, and there at low tide, on a sandy beach at the northern end of Tomales Bay, were the tracks of a good-sized black bear, pristine and perfect in the damp sand. The bear had been moving down the beach before dawn, when the tide was higher and came to a barrier cliff. I could clearly see where it stopped and rocked back and forth, deciding what to do, before it headed up into the forest to go around.

This track sighting was followed over the next several days with reports, and even scat samples, from locations across Marin's southern landscape, where it was feeding heavily on the ripening wax myrtle berries and huckleberries, which were obvious in the scat. My question was: how did it get to the beach? All the usual black bear sightings are well to the north of this area, but not beyond believable dispersal distances. Did it walk six miles south to the foot of the bay and then back up to where we found its tracks, or did it swim the three quarters of a mile across the bay to reach these berry thickets? It became a sacred question. Would it swim or walk? I filed it away and waited for answers.

A month later I was hiking in the Sierra Nevada, and as if in direct answer to my sacred question, I watched a black bear on a distant shore leap into a lake and swim a good half-mile to the other side of a long channel. Shortly after my return, even more "coincidentally," a good friend related a tale of having just seen a black bear swim a mile to an island in the Great Lakes. Not long after that, I watched an elk swim the quarter of a mile across the middle of Abbotts Lagoon, apparently using the quick route. Studying opossums, I was surprised to read that they will sometimes swim a hundred yards to cross a body of water!

Clearly, our bear could easily have crossed the bay. On a still, warm, moonlit night, I'd be tempted to myself.

The power in these sacred questions lies in the sense of aliveness that comes with an open mind and great curiosity, and the satisfaction and surprise when a long-standing question is finally answered. There is magic in how answers are evoked by holding questions this way; there is joy in feeling more connected to the land by simple wondering. As with so many aspects of tracking, keeping a list of questions becomes a part of the fabric of your life. I eventually developed a simple habit of writing these questions down in a small notebook every time I go out, and I try to answer them as soon as I get home and can do some research. This has become one of my primary learning tools.

May 2011

Acting Squirrelly

If you walk through our Douglas fir forests in the spring, you may notice occasional spots where the trails are carpeted with layers of small, green fir cone scales. It's a beautiful and impressive sign of California gray squirrel feeding. I have seen it in years past, but this year the scale piles are much larger and more common—an indication that our local squirrels are doing particularly well.

I began stopping for a while near these litter piles, to watch what would happen, feeling sure that the time would be well spent. Soon enough, especially just after dawn and before dusk, the squirrels would resume their business above me: scolding, calling, chasing, and feeding in a burst of action and motion. Before long, a rain of fir scales would start falling as the squirrels began tearing cones apart high up in the branches.

One detail that had already caught my attention was the conspicuous absence of cones or their cores on the ground, meaning the squirrels were not cutting the cones from the tree before feeding on them as they do in the fall. This spring, they were clearly de-scaling them up in the branches and eating the newly forming nuts up there. Whew! What an appetite for those bitter, turpentine-flavored fruits, extra sappy so early in the year. But eat them they do, with apparent gusto.

One day, while inspecting a particularly prolific scattering, I noticed a heap of small, thin strips of bark amongst the cone scales. Picking some up for closer examination, the inner surface of every strip was covered with a pattern of faint diagonal double stripes about one-eighth inch wide. It was the squirrels' incisor tooth marks. They were cutting the strips and scraping off the sugar-rich inner cambium layer before dropping them to the ground.

I wanted to see what the site on the tree trunks looked like where they stripped the bark, so I climbed the tree. Sure enough, about forty feet up, I found numerous large, bare patches on the trunk and surrounding branches where the bark had been chewed away.

This is springtime behavior. The newborns are learning the ways of the trees, safe from ground predators. The fir cones are starting to ripen, certain trees producing bigger crops and sweeter sap. This new growth is a welcome addition to fall supplies that were cached on the ground and used up during the winter.

The intense social interactions of gray squirrels give rise to a constant flurry of territorial scenting, chew marking, and defensive posturing, illustrating a principle that is common throughout nature: everyday tasks are imbued with multiple meanings. The squirrels create territorial chew marks in certain areas, adding to them regularly and rubbing them with scent from the glands on their cheeks as a message to would-be competitors. Some of these chews are maintained for decades, through generations of the same family, in the same large trees. The markings can grow to immense sizes. The largest I've ever seen was on a huge ponderosa pine in the Sierras. It was a scar over fifteen feet tall, cutting through at least twenty years of annual growth rings! The scar was covered with drying sap leaking out of the exposed inner bark layers. It was startling to see and hard to imagine that squirrels could do that much damage to a tree trunk, but the tooth marks covering the scar edges were proof. The tree itself was doing fine.

In spring, male squirrels form strict hierarchies, fighting to be in position when a female comes into her brief estrus, perhaps for only eight hours in the whole year. A female can lead a whole entourage of males on long, wild chases through trees. This constant social repositioning and territorial boundary-keeping, along with relentless feeding to maintain their high metabolisms, accounts for their noisy and obvious activity.

Gray squirrels' spectacular tails, for which they are named (their genus, *Sciurus*, means "shade-tail"), also serve several purposes: a blanket when it is cold, a parachute in case of a fall, a balancer on leaps and dashes through branches, and a very effective signaling device to warn each other of approaching predators. We are probably all familiar with their repetitive "kuk-kuk-kuk" calls, which they use in coordination with tail flicking to challenge competitors or warn neighbors of potential danger. An afternoon walk through a forest can be filled with these calls, sounding like birdcalls, but with un-bird-like incessantness.

Though they have found relative safety in the trees from ground predators, gray squirrels are still very vulnerable to owls and hawks. They are on constant alert, quick to flag any threat, and they disappear into secondary nests and thickets when an alert becomes an alarm.

Summer brings a shift in eating habits, indicated by the appearance of the cores of fir cones in the litter of scales below feeding trees. As the cones mature, the squirrels begin to sever the whole cone and strip it, rotating it in their front paws like corn on the cob, dropping the core to the ground when they are done. As summer progresses into fall, they begin cutting off and dropping whole cone-covered branch tips and dashing down to strip the cones there and start their seasonal food caching.

At this time of the year, gray squirrels spend a lot of time on the ground. Trees provide safety and nesting, but their primary food, particularly in Bear Valley, consists of fir cones, bay nuts, and oak acorns, all of which they harvest off the ground in the fall. They descend through well-established routes and fan out over the ground to collect them. In the fall, they both feed directly on the nuts on the ground and also cache them for later. Then, in the late winter and spring, they spend a great deal of time foraging to rediscover their caches and dig the seeds out. You can watch them busily searching around, sniffing the ground incessantly, finding little patches of caches, scratching through the leaves down into the soil to unearth the seeds, happily filling themselves up on the treasure. They find these caches with an excellent spatial memory and a sharp sense of smell.

When you come across one, you find small, flat-bottomed digs, about two inches square and just barely dug through the humus layer into the mineral soil beneath. The throw-mound of leaves and topsoil, all in one direction, is square shaped, where their fast little front feet have pulled the soil between their large back feet.

This is perhaps where their erratic movements have given birth to our term for someone with a flaky and unpredictable nature—someone who acts a little squirrelly. But in the wisdom of evolution, this comical and endearing behavior has multiple advantages. The herky-jerky bounding motion is designed to be unpredictable to a potential predator. Without it, squirrels would be too vulnerable during the fall and winter months, when they spend so much time on the ground, far from the safety of their trees.

Their maddening hop-and-stop, this-way-and-that motion also confuses thieves that threaten to steal the newly cached seeds. Often, if you sit still long enough, you can see the squirrels making phony caches, false digs a short distance from the actual cache, to throw off spies. And, like old misers, they continually reshuffle their caches, counting and re-hiding their treasure. A single squirrel can store thousands of seeds and nuts—and is able to recover ninety percent of them during the winter. They use a "scatter-hoarding" strategy, increasing the odds of sufficient winter food supplies by spreading it out widely. In fact, quite a bit of give and take goes on with these scattered caches; you could call it thievery or, more altruistically, neighborly support, but they will often harvest someone else's caches.

This iconic friend, so relentlessly obvious and yet mysterious in so many ways, was hunted nearly to extinction by around 1900, when a century of unregulated hunting and a perverse killing mania had run much of wildlife in America to the brink of extinction. I've read reports of populations of squirrels in the millions in the eastern hardwood forests, so many that they were noted occasionally, as late as the 1850s, to suddenly go en masse, hundreds of thousands of them, on long dispersal migrations. Lemming-like, they would form blankets crossing the land and anything in the way, even rivers.

They seemed limitless to European colonizers, who only saw this abundance as another resource to exploit. Hunters out at the edges of civilization, at mining and railroad building camps, would shoot hundreds a day, year after year, to feed the work crews. It seemed like there would always be more a little further on. Until it didn't.

Luckily, a conservation movement was born, and is still making headway against unsustainable habits of contemporary human culture. The hope and humor that a squirrel provides can be an inspiration to continue our push to rebuild our Garden of Eden here on earth.

August 2012

The Nature of Spirit

What is the nature of the spirit in the spirit of nature? There is an aspect of tracking, and of knowing ourselves, that involves spirit; yet as we know, spirit is impossible to define. It is beyond the logic of description. There are many aspects of spirit, which is partly what makes it so difficult to talk about. Many individuals have gotten the concept so confused that they will insist there is no such thing as spirit. Others will hold to their own belief system as if it is the only truth. This is largely the effect of coming from a culture that confuses regional religions with spirituality, and is willing to go to war over the differences. But if you are reading about tracking, right now, chances are you know that spirit is truly universal and runs through all things on earth. But what is it? It is a tricky question to answer with language.

Let's go tracking and find out!

There we are, following the fresh-looking footsteps of a young doe through a mixed oak and pine forest so typical of our coastal slopes and ridges. The tracks are simply roughed-up anomalies in the settled pattern of the leafy debris on the forest floor. Close inspection reveals creases and tears in the leaves and needles where the doe stepped with her hooves. We can see that she walked through here very recently, while the ground was damp from yesterday's rain. There are none of the sharp cracks and breaks that we would have found in the dry conditions a few days ago. The closer we look and let our eyes adjust, the more apparent the tracks are. After a while, tiny details that were invisible at first come into focus, the shapes of the hooves obvious in the leaves. Yet no matter how carefully we observe them, the tracks remain lifeless and tell us little about the animal who made them.

Now touch a track, slow your mind down, shift into a wider vision that sees the patterns as well as the details, shift into the present. Let yourself fall into the context of the situation. Include yourself, and me, in the picture: There we are in the forest on Mount Wittenberg, on a beautiful winter morning. There's a chill in the air. Low-angled sunlight splashes through the branches of the trees. The damp ground smells pungent and earthy.

Widening our awareness, while still touching the tracks, we begin to feel the spirit of the deer. We are connecting with her. We can sense her caution as she approached the edge of the trees, drawn to the meadow beyond where she intended to browse, and the increasing care with which she placed each foot, the pauses as she listened and strained to see ahead.

We are entering her spirit, we can feel her life force and the web of her existence: her feeding routine; her familiarity with this territory where she has grown up and foraged every day of her life; her family, part of her protective sphere; the familiar sounds and smells; the patterns of bird calls; and the rustle of leaves in the breeze. She was a little drowsy, having fed well during the night, under the moonlight; after a little more foraging, she was ready to find a warm spot to lie down, to doze and digest. There is just such a spot on the other side of the little meadow. Yet she knew, no matter how sleepy she felt, she must always keep some primal part of herself on alert, ready to bolt in an instant at the approach of danger.

We feel the tracks, sink deeper until we are a part of her. We sense her thoughts and feelings. We see a faint luminous glow in her trail, impossible to explain in words, but clearly very fresh. Through the tiniest observations, we see the tiny indicators that identify her tracks from all the others under the trees. The pacing, the size of her feet and how she places them, the weight, the shape of her hoof edges, and the age of these tracks attest to this. All of this provides a factual backup for what we feel in spirit.

As we already know by now, she moved out from under the cover of the trees and into the meadow. We knew that before we looked, because for a moment we had become a part of her and a part of the forest. As we expand our spirit and join with the earth, these things become strangely clear. The earth beckons us, and we feel it calling. We recognize that deep, pleasing sense of release when we respond to it. We've done it a million times since we were born, testing it over and over, finding the patterns in the deep recesses of our subconscious minds. When we let go of our hesitations and give ourselves over to these feelings, we are flooded with a strange sense of giddy joy, a laughter that bubbles up from deep in our belly, the surest sign that we are on the track of the truth. We want to follow this feeling.

Yet, as modern humans, living in the grip of our logical minds, we have also learned to disregard many of these feelings, often dismissing them as mere "imagination," when indeed they are the very voices of the creator, of the spirit of the earth, of our most ancient ancestry, speaking directly to us. It takes practice to differentiate this subtle voice from our mental chatter, to listen to it and to believe it in spite of our logical mind, which may rebel and try to dominate our thinking.

We've been moving very slowly and quietly, almost to the point of invisibility. So absorbed in the details have we become that now, looking up and listening again, we realize that the morning birdcalls around us have picked up to a pleasant intensity and have a busy ring to them. The birds have returned to baseline and are going about their business, feeding while the morning is still sweet. They've pretty much forgotten about us. Silently and very slowly, we crawl to the edge of the trees, not realizing that without a word or a thought, we've dropped into a deep silent stalk, a sense of electric expectation filling us even as we work to stay calm and remain in this state of harmony.

We take seemingly forever to crawl the last few paces and slowly peek our heads out from behind the leafy screen . . . and there she is, so close we could reach out and touch her back legs. From this perspective, she looks huge, potentially dangerous. For a moment we are disconcerted, worried that we have just put ourselves into danger. This is a strong, healthy wild animal, with sharp hooves. We can sense her tremendous primal power. But she is looking the other way, reaching down to munch a few leaves, looking back up while she chews them, the stems hanging loosely out of the corners of her mouth, her ears constantly swiveling, taking in the story in the language of the birds and the shifts of the wind. She is very relaxed. The birds have not given us away!

She slowly wanders across the little pocket of meadow, a last munch here and there, toward a loose patch of brush on a sunny knob, where we already knew she was headed. Honoring her, we remain quiet and still, filled with the sense of respect and restraint that this level of connection calls for. Touching a track can evoke all of this and far more when we allow the earth to speak. All we really need to do is listen to step into that deep pool, the realm of spirit.

January 2010

Population Dynamics: Badgers, Voles, Gophers, and Coyotes

Part 1: The Badger and the Vole

The symphony of life in the wildlands, rhythmic and complex, plays out in accordance with the restless and ever-changing weather patterns. Wet years, dry years; early winters, late winters; cold years, warm years. Life evolved in these unpredictable patterns over the course of a billion years. What we see is what worked, what held up through changing times. Nature is amazingly responsive and adaptable. Common prey animals, such as brush rabbits, field voles, deer mice, and pocket gophers, are particularly responsive to changing environmental conditions and cycle through population swings.

A few years ago, after two long and steady rainy seasons that stoked lush grass growth, vole populations exploded throughout our coastal hills and fields. Their little surface runs, their feeding stations (small mown porches at their tunnel openings), and their scat accumulations were easy to spot in any ungrazed field. But over the last three years of scant rainfall, the grassy habitats began to dry up. The voles, overpopulated for strained conditions, resorted to eating the bark of lupine shrubs. As large swaths of lupines began to die back, botanists feared their decline. But the deep-rooted lupines survived the onslaught and have mostly recovered as rainfall has increased, having evolved, over eons, to account for these rhythms.

But what are voles anyway? Everyone is familiar with mice, from Mickey Mouse to the ubiquitous house mouse in our attics and pantries. You don't hear as much about voles, commonly called field mice, but they are universally present, often in great numbers, in every grassy habitat. They eat strictly fresh vegetation (unlike the omnivorous deer mouse, which caches dry food), so they are not attracted to our houses. But they do require thick structural vegetation for cover. If you part the cover and look within, you will see a maze of little winding half-tunnels on the ground surface where they zip along like little race cars in their tracks, their flexible bodies zooming around corners, barely slowing down, speed one of their primary defenses as they travel from feeding areas to burrows. If you stop and sit down quietly in a busy vole meadow at dawn or dusk, you will soon see them flitting between clumps of grass in little flashes.

This small, mouse-like creature is one of the most prolific rodents on Earth. Their populations rise and fall with the rhythms of grasslands. Here is the magic of how a population boom can happen: as with most animals, both size and frequency of vole litters goes up in good conditions and down in poor. A single vole can produce anywhere from five to ninety offspring in one year. The potential population increase is exponential, because each of those young can reproduce seven to eight weeks after birth.

Implied here is the profound importance they serve as a food source for predators. A wide array of predators must eat an enormous number of them just to keep a semblance of balance in the system. But as quickly as their populations can increase, just as quickly can they decline, ever so sensitive to food supply and predation. Similarly, predators may have more and larger litters in good years and fewer, smaller litters in poor ones. Voles are truly the base of the food pyramid for carnivores, and the recent vole collapse was a big loss for all of our rodent hunters, from bobcats and foxes to red-tailed hawks and owls, leading to their own population slumps.

Yet one unlikely predator not only held its ground during the drought, but thrived and increased to numbers I had never seen before: the badger! Usually reclusive and nocturnal, the badger is a fossorial hunter—it digs for ground-dwelling prey. It works like a typical predator, roaming a large territory that is often passed from parents to children, moving from one zone to another, taking the easy pickings then moving on, employing a deep understanding of the territory.

Here on the coast, badgers specialize in hunting pocket gophers, and, as gardeners in West Marin know all too well, gophers have done very well during the drought. Any good gopher habitat in this area, open sloping fields with good sun exposure and drainage, has been utterly riddled with gopher digs, sometimes literally covered with their tailings. In itself, this has been an amazing development to witness. But there were other, more mysterious diggings.

Last year, I began to notice more and more huge burrows, nearly a foot wide and bottomless, in grassy fields—grazed and ungrazed—throughout the area: badger digs. In the fields near the park headquarters and the neighboring model Coast Miwok Indian village, Kule Loklo, I found dozens of fresh large digs. In the fields near the foot of Tomales Bay, where normally only an occasional badger dig can be found, their work spread to all corners of the preserve, even in the low flatlands close to the marsh edges. Near Abbotts Lagoon, more and more digs were appearing in the plowed fields, scattered evenly across the land. Even along trail edges and roadsides, huge burrows and mounds appeared.

I began getting calls from neighbors: "What could be making these huge holes in my yard?" Each inspection revealed the same pattern: two or three large, downward spiraling holes, eight to ten inches in diameter, ramping down at a shallow angle, with three- to four-foot throw-mounds full of large rocks and clods, and up to ten or fifteen smaller, messier digs surrounding the burrows—a classic badger dig. It is pretty easy to tell which hole is freshest; often that one will have the telltale pigeon-toed tracks leading into the hole but not coming out. Badger digs in backyards! This never happened before. Something profound had changed.

The situation led to a lot of questions. Why so many holes, and why are they spreading into the neighborhoods? What do those holes mean? How do badgers live? Where do they sleep? How many gophers does a badger eat? Who is making all the small digs and why? Are the badgers hunting voles too? How, in fact, does a badger catch a gopher?

More questions, from the other side of the equation: How do gophers really live, anyway? How fast can gophers reproduce? How can they thrive so well during a drought? How big is a gopher territory? How many gophers live in one area?

And what about the coyotes who roam these same fields? How does a coyote dig differ from a badger dig? Coyotes commonly hunt gophers too. Coyotes are masters of sniffing out live gophers in fresh runs as well as hearing the gophers in their underground nest chambers, where they will dig them out.

Part 2: The Gopher

Observation and research finally yielded some clear answers and a few theories about how these lives are related and what the drought has revealed.

First, a little gopher biology: Our local pocket gophers, despite the colony-like appearance of a hillside riddled with holes, are solitary animals who vigorously defend their own territory. They maintain a system of runs leading to feeding areas; preferring green vegetation, they eat the roots or pull whole plants underground, occasionally roaming out from the mouths of their runs to nibble on surface grasses, temporarily storing the cuttings in their fur-lined cheek "pockets." Their nest chambers are lined with large masses of soft, dry grasses, usually one to three feet deep. In ideal conditions, here on the coast, they can give birth to four or five litters in a year, with up to twelve young in each litter, potentially sixty young in a year.

A single gopher territory can be as small as twenty-five feet in diameter; what looks like a colony may actually be a series of adjoining, interlocking territories, shaped and sized according to the landscape and plant patterns. A gopher's territory is a prized set of assets: a run system leading to fertile feeding areas, several food caches, and one or two nest chambers. Boundaries are maintained by scent markings and shows of aggression, and gophers are well aware of their neighbors. Despite the effectiveness of their fossorial strategy, gophers are heavily hunted by a wide variety of predators and have high rates of attrition. But within hours of a predation, neighboring gophers will annex and re-occupy any vacated territory. It is a dynamic situation.

When conditions become crowded, young gophers embark on long overland dispersal journeys to establish new territories. Last winter, in perfect dawn conditions, I tracked one gopher who made a half-mile journey across open sand during the moonless night, toward chaparral-covered slopes, without ever breaking its steady trot! At last, as it neared its destination, in the last twenty feet or so, its tracks began to show little toe drags, revealing that the tired gopher, seeing the end of its journey, was finally letting its guard down slightly. This year in particular, due to both the drought and overpopulation, gophers were in a long and intense dispersal cycle, giving me the opportunity to become much more familiar with their tracks.

From my observations, I think there were two keys to the success of gophers in the drought. First, the vole populations crashed quickly with the failure of grasses (and possibly intensified predation), leaving less competition for food they share with the gophers. And second, in spite of the drought, several species of perennial plant tubers and bulbs were able to thrive, providing gophers with a steady food source late into the dry season. One indication of this was the increasing amount of bulb husks mixed into the balls of the gophers' nest grasses, when revealed by coyote or badgers digs.

Whatever the causes, the gopher population increased dramatically over the last two to three years. In response, the badger population spiked. Two things you can count on: the more ideal the conditions, the higher their birth and survival rate; and the more burrows you see, the higher their population. This population spike inevitably led to an unusual amount of badger dispersal this year, as the young moved out to explore new habitat in the hopes of establishing their own territories. All those backyard digs were simply explorations, the reclusive young badgers testing the benefits of new territory at the edges of human habitation, hunting as they explored.

Here is what the badger is doing: each night, the stout fellow emerges from his hole as darkness gathers, sits at the top of the throw-mound, and spends a while cleaning himself and attuning to the sounds and smells of the evening before setting out for a night of opportunistic foraging, focusing primarily on gophers. By sound and smell, a badger can locate an active burrow system and find either the active nesting chamber or the run where the gopher is presently feeding. This member of the weasel family, with his huge front claws and webbed back feet, is capable of digging small holes in seconds and deep burrows in minutes. With its primal predator focus, the badger will find an active gopher and set to work with instant frenzy.

The large digs, spiraling down at a shallow angle, usually aim for the jackpot of gopher hunting: the nest with a bunch of noisy babies. After feasting on this treasure, the badger may simply continue digging down to create a safe and secure bed to sleep in during the day. If the area is teeming with gophers, the badger may stay for a few days, hunting the peripheral gophers who reoccupy the space, before moving on, but they seldom use a burrow for more than two or three days, which accounts for the profusion of holes where they regularly hunt. They are restless, opportunistic predators constantly moving on to easier pickings in the next meadow.

A typical badger dig has one, two, sometimes three very deep spiraling holes, with giant throw-mounds revealing the amount of material that was dug out. Surrounding these large holes are usually several smaller digs, sometimes called probe holes. Here, the badger is hunting in newly dug gopher tunnels, shallow cul-de-sacs where the gopher is feeding.

The strategy is to trap the gopher in one of those dead ends where the badger can dig up the gopher faster than the gopher can dig to get away. Coyotes, as well as some domestic dogs, can do this too. With each probe dig, the badger is mapping out the gopher's tunnel system and working his way closer to the hot-smelling, active gopher. The badger may actually be herding the gopher into a dead end, or at least that is the net effect.

Roughly speaking, if one grown badger eats two gophers a night, that's a lot of gophers—sixty per month! And a lot of badger holes. If a successful pair of badgers produces two litters of four in an excellent year, you've got ten badgers consuming several hundred gophers per month! Add in the other gopher predators: the red-tailed hawks and harriers, the coyotes, foxes and bobcats, weasels and skunks, gopher snakes and rattlers. Then add more prey: the voles, mice, brush rabbits, birds, snakes, and frogs. It is mind-boggling how many animals are being consumed in the ongoing dance of life and abundance. But that indeed is what is going on out in our fields. It is the definition of healthy equilibrium.

Part 3: The Coyote

Now, what about the role of the coyote in all this badger activity? Both predators love to dig up gopher nests, and their holes are similar sizes, about eight to ten inches in diameter. But there are several ways to tell them apart, with the differences in their digging patterns tied to their respective morphologies.

The badger, with its short legs and low-slung body, digs at a relatively shallow angle, kicking the soil out behind itself with its partially webbed back feet; usually the badger hole quickly begins spiraling. They dig speedily, soil flying furiously behind them as they quickly disappear into the ground. With its inward-turned legs and flattened body, it makes a horizontal, flattened hole. With their long claws and powerful arms, they are able to remove rocks larger than softballs, and their large throw-mound is usually in only one direction.

The coyote, on the other hand, digs like a dog, standing on its long back legs while reaching into the hole with its front paws to excavate in a paddling style, pulling the soil out and discharging it through their back legs. They will often work their way around the edges of the hole, spraying the soil in all directions. They tend to make a vertical, narrow hole, without the messy probe holes around the main dig, and leave a much smaller throw-mound because they are only digging down to the nest. With its lighter-duty digging equipment, the coyote doesn't dig out rocks much larger than its own foot.

We have a rare opportunity right now to see an unusual and impressive natural feature: badger holes sprinkled across our grassy landscapes. Make time in your busy life to stop and enjoy such phenomena while they last. A good life is built of just such moments! If you find one, stand back, consider the overall pattern, and look for neighboring digs. When you find the dried grass balls of a dug-up gopher nest, look closely: you can see what the gophers have been eating. Peek at the sidewalls of the hole, where you can often find grooves left by the badger's large digging claws.

But always, above all, I encourage you to be respectful in your studies. Give the natives some space. Be careful with your own impact. Be as invisible and nondisruptive to animals as possible, even while using tracking and awareness skills to get in close amongst them.

December 2013

The Evaluation

Tracking in the real world often involves a lot of guessing and conjecture; it is very challenging to commit to a final answer. But when a situation forces you to decide, you look very closely, draw on everything you've ever learned and everything you can see in the landscape, the location, the habitat, and the season. You run down your mental checklists, considering all possibilities, forced to stretch your knowledge as far as possible. You learn one of the most important rules of tracking: when you've got the right answer, all the parts fit. When you find yourself stretching too many details to make it suit your guess, you're probably wrong.

The Marin Tracking Club had the good fortune recently to host our first International Tracker Evaluation. This test, the only one of its kind in the world, objectively grades the skill of animal trackers. It was developed by a South African, Louis Leibenberg, who saw the growing ecotourism industry in Africa as a way to keep the old tracking skills from dying out. As he searched for trackers to meet the growing demand, it became apparent that a rating system was necessary, since many men claimed to be trackers but few really knew the art. He developed an intense two-day process, now known as the Tracker Eval. Mark Elbroch, one of the leading trackers in the U.S. and the author of some of the best tracking guides available, became a certified evaluator and has been conducting the test in North America for several years. When we heard that Mark was offering an Eval in Marin, we quickly signed up.

Over two days, we worked in several locations with different habitats: sand dunes near the coast, bishop pine forests on the Inverness Ridge, and riparian zones along an inland creek. Mark and his assistant, Casey McFarland, himself an author of a wonderful feather identification guide, would explore ahead, find various tracks and signs, circle them, and ask very simple questions: "Who made this track?" "What gait is it in?" "Which foot is it?" "Who nibbled this branch?" "Who made this scat?" These two guys track and test all over the country; they really know their stuff. They've seen coyote tracks from the snows in New England to the deserts of Arizona and mink tracks from Wyoming to California.

A score is kept for each participant, awarding higher credit for correct answers to difficult questions, and higher penalties for incorrect answers to easy questions. The results are balanced and converted to a final score from 1 to 100. A score in the 70s gives a Class I rating, the 80s earns a Class II, the 90s a Class III and 100 earns a Specialist rating.

It is all conducted at a slow, relaxed pace. There is plenty of time for each question. But it is serious: no prompting, sharing, or hinting. Answers are carefully whispered to the scorekeepers so everybody has a fair chance. Pushed to your limits, your resulting score is an accurate gauge of your skill. But the best part of the test is the education you receive. Mark and Casey take time to review each section of tracks, explaining in detail what they see and what tiny details and contextual clues are the keys to the correct answers. It is a valuable session with two of the best trackers in the country.

Our group as a whole made one of the highest scores of any group Mark has evaluated, validating the quality of our tracking program.

But it was humbling to learn how far we have yet to go and where the edges of our knowledge lay.

My edges, at that time, were clearly in the realm of bird tracks. I've been studying bird tracks for some time, comparing the minute differences between birds of a similar class, such as sparrows and towhees, and studying gait patterns, feeding signs, skeletal differences, feather identification, and scat and pellet identification. It's a large realm, very different than the mammal world. It takes me more time to absorb and retain the information, to understand how the morphological details of birds relate to their niches. Birds are more highly specialized for particular niches, while mammals seem more adaptable to wider ranges of conditions.

I found that my lack of thorough knowledge compromised my ability to actually see the tracks themselves. I was surprised to find that in some cases, I couldn't see complete tracks until Mark pointed them out, when all of a sudden they popped into view. This is an aspect of tracking and perception that I find endlessly fascinating: we simply can't see something when we don't have a mental image or concept of it.

On the other hand, I did very well at some other edges of my experience. I successfully identified the right front track of a deer mouse in the sandy mud under a bridge along the creek. In the perfect substrate I could see, in the quarter-inch track, the four little dots of the palm and heel pads and the typical angles of the toes. But in reviewing it, Mark pointed out an even tinier detail that is a final identifier—an extremely faint fifth dot, the track of the vestigial thumb.

Another challenging question involved where two coyotes crossed paths on the coast. The question was: which trail is freshest? Which one came first and which one followed? One set, probably male, was a little larger, and the grains of sand in the floor of the tracks looked slightly drier and looser than the smaller tracks of the female. A first glance would lead one to the conclusion that the male had gone first. But additional details that led to a different conclusion. It is pretty technical, but see if you can stay with it.

Right where the trails crossed each other, two tracks slightly overlapped. The following coyote had stepped right next to one of the lead coyote's tracks. A small crust of sand, the size of a quarter, had been pushed out from the side of the male's track when he shifted direction. This plate touched the toe of the female track. At first glance it looked as if the female had stepped on the edge of the plate, cutting part of it off, meaning that she would have been following. But closer observation showed that the plate from the larger track, the male's, had pushed over the female's track, meaning it was later. The ragged edge in the plate was not caused by the female stepping on it. It was caused by the plate actually bumping into and being disrupted by the edge of the female's track!

That is small stuff! Seeing this, I had to conclude that the male had come after the female. There was some disagreement and it was a difficult call, but Casey thought it was clear; I got that one right. Now, whenever I encounter this situation, it is fairly obvious to me.

A final lesson, in the bishop pine forest above Shell Beach, considered a small pine bough that had fallen to the forest floor. It had been cut off from its branch and the needles on one side had been sheared off evenly with clean angled cuts. The question—who did all this?—had a two-part answer.

Gray squirrels had chewed off the branch, with characteristic incisor tooth marks on the stub, a conclusion corroborated by numerous pinecone cores strewn about. At certain times of the year, squirrels cut off branch tips with cones on them, dropping them to the ground and descending to dismantle them and eat the nuts. But brush rabbits had sheared the needles after the branch had fallen to the ground, a part of their diet I had not known about. The lesson: don't automatically assume that two closely related signs come from the same animal.

All in all, the real gains I made from this test stemmed from the intensive studies we did in preparing for it, and in the reviews after each section, especially the reviews of the ones I got wrong. This kind of knowledge, once gained in actual field discovery, is never lost again, so the sense of growth and accumulation is strong and steady.

May 2010

The Disappearance: July

In an unusual drought year, the unusual patterns continue. Something seemed amiss this late June and early July, after the unexpectedly exuberant spring.

Indeed, in a period that typically might have seen thirty inches of rain, we had seven! As February approached, normally a wet and verdant time, our hills were bare dirt piles instead of lush green carpets of new grasses. The clock never started ticking. In my sixty-plus years, I'd never seen this happen. There was no First Awakening in October, no Second Awakening in January; everything was on hold. An eerie feeling gripped the land, a dry cold.

Finally the skies broke open in late February and we were drenched with ten inches of rain, followed by a series of wet storms every two to three weeks into early June; better late than never. Nature provided optimum conditions for growth: a warming earth and lots of evenly spaced rain just as the days were growing longer. Revealing that she has been through these kinds of cycles many millions of times, Mother Earth was prepared with a great diversity of plant and animal species who responded to the rain with immediate action. Life was renewed. Everything burst into accelerated growth, like watching time-lapse photography.

Grasses grew tall in weeks, quickly heading up to seed. Insects, amphibians, birds, and mammals all compressed their mating cycles into the shortened spring. It looked like there was one shot, and everybody took it. Coyote families howled every night. Birds sang loud and insistently as they set up nesting territories in the brush and forests. Frog ponds roared. Insects hatched. Mosquitos swarmed! A normally four- or five-month cycle was squeezed into two months of reproductive frenzy.

Then suddenly . . . quiet. Late June. Early summer. Only a sporadic single coyote call at night. The birds stopped singing and were gone. Gray foxes, so often seen dashing across roads at night, seemed to have vanished. Even tracks were scarce in some of the tracking club's most reliable study areas. The bottom had dropped out. Normal patterns were abandoned.

Where'd everybody go? It was as if the animals had all gone into hiding.

In this shortened spring, reproductive cycles overlapped more than usual. After advertising for mates and claiming territories at an accelerated pace in the spring, there was a compressed birthing season. Animals seemed to sense that they might only have one chance this year. There was not enough time to spread out the way citizens of the natural world tend to do. It was as if everyone was tending their young at once, keeping a low profile, hiding under the radar, trying to stay alive and get the kids launched.

All attention focused on the business of gathering food and feeding babies. Being unusually compressed, the shift into summer was more noticeable this year than most. Like the brief spring, there was a feeling in the air that summer would be short too. I could feel it. Nature could feel it. I've never seen or felt anything like this here before. The summer pause in the animal world is normal, but usually so subtle that we miss it. This year, the effect was magnified.

Now, however, in early July, a new frenzy has begun. What a choppy year! Suddenly everyone is out again, feeding, growing, fattening up on the summer abundance while they can. Along the shorelines, I've noticed a big boom in tracks—coyote trails looping around and around, deer crossing busily from one feeding area to another. Skunks, who disappeared for the last month or two, are out in their erratically wandering forays, rabbits are darting back and forth, nibbling their patches of greenery, and bobcats are steadily plying their solitary routes, scat-marking their boundaries and claims. To feed the growing kids now, everyone is spreading further out.

Families of birds are fledging young and spreading out, foraging, calling to each other as they sweep through the landscape on their rounds. Insects are exploding from larval stages started in late winter and early spring, providing a burst of protein for just about everyone. Huckleberries began ripening early, some as early as May on the ridge tops, and the foxes took immediate advantage.

Birds are spending more time on the ground. Great horned owls are making long ground journeys in their unique way of walking, very straight lines veering at sharp angles, to track down their next beetle. It's one of my favorite tracks: big right and left K-shaped impressions, walking that revs up to a run. Ravens walk on the ground a lot too, a hundred yards sometimes, lurching from one prey objective to another, leaving their signature long rear-toe claw drags and their rolling, curvy trails, reminding me of a sailor swaggering down the deck.

Raccoons are foraging along all of the shorelines and carrying their prizes back to hidden spots in the dunes where they can eat unmolested. Food is king, and anyone who has some is fair game for harassment.

In this first week or two of July, summer seems at least a month early this year. It is more like late August. How is the rest of the season going to play out? It is impossible to predict, particularly with our highly varied microclimates and our strong marine influence, but I expect fewer and smaller litters in general. It may really dry up again. Late fall can be a difficult time for animals that can't migrate, perhaps more so this year. Starvation is a sad but necessary part of life and death in nature, much like predation. It is a fundamental aspect of evolution. Like brutal winters in northern latitudes, dry summers can be the cleaver in this Mediterranean climate, separating those who are capable of making it from those who can't. Natural animal populations instinctively respond to drought and other tight conditions by lowering birth rates, but it is never a perfect balance.

For now though, we have a rare opportunity to watch as the shortened spring rapidly transforms into high summer. Forests, meadows, and hillsides are richly textured with luxurious plant growth and kaleidoscopic hues of green. The waters, beaches, and wetlands are rich with fish, crustaceans, and other invertebrates, and shore birds are finding plenty of food. The waters are warming while the early summer fogs prevent the world from drying out too fast. It is a good time to be alive.

August 2015

Baring My Sole: A Lesson from Ishi

I've always been fascinated by the story of Ishi, the last surviving member of his Northern California tribe, the Yahi. The fate of his people, after thousands of years of stable life, was doomed by the discovery of gold in their streams, which precipitated one of the most wanton pulses of genocide in human history. An unimaginably long-standing and sustainable culture was all but obliterated within a few decades. Christianity was the justification, at the time, for the genocide (of "sub-human heathens"), while greed—gold fever and a land grab—was the real motivation. Superior force was all that was required to do it. Ishi was one of the last links to the quickly disappearing native culture.

West Marin had no gold, but the results were much the same, as they were throughout the Americas. Who knows what kind of atrocities were committed right here by our own forebears, only a few generations ago, to clear these lands of their original inhabitants? The details have largely, and conveniently, been forgotten, but the tragedy remains and the crimes go unrectified, a legacy we all carry.

Ironically, it has been surmised that, in a form of the biological principle known as "resource partitioning," Ishi's people, living a simple subsistence lifestyle, could have coexisted with the miners and ranchers to this day with no discernible competition or interference. The cultural arrogance and violence of European colonizers is hard to comprehend, but what amazes me is how those hunter-gatherers stayed with their way of life and the traditions they loved until the very end, despite the potential and possibly tantalizing advantages of the "civilized" agricultural and industrial world intruding upon them. Even when only three members of his tribe were left—himself, his mother, and his uncle—Ishi's family observed traditional seasonal ceremonies of thankfulness for the gifts of the earth and the creator, building one last sweat lodge for purification and prayer. Clearly, they had witnessed the violent side of our culture and did not see a path for themselves in that direction. It is possible that, coming from a stable way of life that had held up for millennia, it was obvious to them that this aggressive new culture was unsustainable, despite its overwhelming power.

Finally, alone and in grief, Ishi walked out of his paradise.

Luckily, he was embraced by Berkeley anthropologist Theodore Kroeber and his family. The warmth and generosity that Ishi shared as he lived his last years in this alien world have, to me, always been a testament to the depth and enduring values embodied in his native culture. He never turned to the darkness of anger, hostility, or hatred. Instead, he projected a joy and adaptability that always impressed those he encountered.

There was one story in this amazing saga that particularly caught my attention, a simple remark I found very intriguing. When told that on the streets of Berkeley he would have to wear shoes, Ishi was surprised and asked: "But how will I know where I am?"

The question is startling, revealing a perspective entirely foreign to us. Contemplating this remark, I finally realized that he asked this question on two levels. Ishi navigated by feeling the ground underfoot. The ground told him where he was and who he was. Feet are incredible mapping and grounding tools, with deep memories.

Feet have obviously evolved in connection with the earth. A feel for the earth is an essential part of awareness. Our feet are designed to walk in contact with the ground, but for modern humans, in divorcing themselves from both the earth and the realms of spirit, walking without shoes is seen as a little weird, even disrespectful.

When I began to study tracking, I realized how difficult it is to walk quietly with shoes on and how liberating it is to be free of the need for shoes. So I committed to relearning the skill. I began walking and running barefoot on trails and beaches and at home as much as possible. It took me nearly five years to really learn how to walk without shoes. But like riding a bike, the skill will not be forgotten once reacquired.

For a couple of years, I beat my feet up, forgetting I didn't have the armor of shoes. I did things feet are not designed for. But as my feet strengthened and I relearned how to walk, I moved differently. I learned to feel the ground. With each step, I reached my feet out slightly, testing the ground with my toes and the ball of my foot before committing my weight to the next step, giving me a critical micro-second to respond to sharp objects.

It is a very slight shift, but critical, natural, part of how we are designed. My whole structural system became more dynamic and flexible. I regained a system of shock absorption from toes to vertebrae. My foot problems disappeared. My knees and back felt better. I realized that those hundreds of muscles in my feet and legs had become weak from all the so-called support of modern shoes; now I was awakening them, and they were responding quickly. I never moved the same way again.

One of the most important benefits of going barefoot is the way it slows you down. You walk more consciously and feel the terrain changing underfoot. Becoming quieter, you hear more of the world around you. With feet and toes gripping the earth, you return to yourself. Remembering where you are, you navigate your inner world with more clarity. I developed a deeper sense of location from the ground—where the bishop pine needles cushion the trails, where the sharp rocks on the ridge are, where the brambles cross the trails, how the ground varies by season. I began to do what Ishi did all his life—unconsciously mapping the world with my feet.

Walking barefoot gave me a greater understanding of how animals move, how they place their feet and respond to the ground. It gave me a new way to understand the finer nuances in tracks and how the earth directs the way an animal moves and the routes it takes. In the Apache tracking tradition that I learned, it is said that the Earth plays an animal like a musical instrument. When I walk our hills barefoot, or with the thinnest of moccasins or water shoes, I can much more clearly hear that music running through me and feel the landscape directing me.

After walking barefoot for some time, the structure of the soles of my feet changed, influencing how I walk. This change is not lost anymore, even when I wear shoes for months in the cold of winter. Rocky trails and gravelly paths are no longer difficult to navigate, no matter how long I've gone without taking my shoes off. I'm just not a tenderfoot anymore. My feet are more sensitive to the feel of the ground, but it is no longer painful, and my mind is more aware of how my feet feel and what they are telling me.

Having learned how to walk on the land without shoes, I make the shift immediately now when going barefoot, slowing down, more conscious of how and where I place my feet. The sense of freedom this brings is worth all the effort to learn the skill. I'm no longer stymied by wet areas, muddy patches, creeks, or streams. It surprises me how daunted shoe-wearers can be when confronted with water. I don't hesitate to take my shoes off and cross. My feet are glad to feel the earth again. It brings more than a hint of the joy and abandon I felt as a child, a greater sense of possibility, a stronger connection with the landscape, and, sometimes, a feeling of connection with the ancient heritage we all share.

November 2009

A Walk to the Beach

It's difficult to get more than six or eight people around a scat or track, so that's typically my cap when I lead tracking walks. But recently I led a field seminar of twenty-five people on a short hike to Kehoe Beach. It was my first experience leading such a large group, and I was nervous, even with the help of my tracking club partners. I was hoping for the excitement of bold, large animal tracks: otter tracks at the mouth of the creek, with their five little teardrop shaped toes, maybe some swirl patterns where they burst from the water onto the shore to roll and slide. Or maybe we'd find the tracks of a coyote scouting the dunes for jackrabbits, showing their shifting gait patterns as they respond to the smells and sounds around them. I wanted something big to allay my worries about how to draw this large group into the subtleties of tracks and nature awareness. So even while we started out, practicing inner quietude as we headed down the trail, I felt impatient to get to the beach and the really "good" stuff.

I started with a little trailhead lesson and the basics of slow walking and open vision, quieting our minds together, toning down our presence and pulling in our rings of disturbance. All of these practices are important for entering the right mindset for tracking. With such a large group, it is even more so. But I was impressed with this group and how well our short lesson at the trailhead set the tone. We started down the trail and moved as one, very quietly and smoothly, everyone excited to see what we'd find at the beach, glancing and talking in hushed murmurs over a few of the things we began to find along the way, a coyote scat or mouse tracks.

The walk out, a trail following a marshy creek, was full of surprises, revelations, and mysteries. We saw a brush rabbit reclining languidly, sunning itself, back legs outstretched, on a warm sandy spot. It allowed the whole group to approach surprisingly close, maybe ten feet, before reluctantly scampering away. We inspected a raccoon latrine on top of an old driftwood log, with scat full of sand crab shells from the surf line—a glimpse of their evening range—and a coyote scat containing pieces of fawn hoof, leaving us wondering if it took the fawn itself or possibly scavenged a bobcat's kill?

There was unusual heavy browsing amongst the lupine, quite unlike deer browse: so this is how elk eat! Song sparrows and goldfinches were dismantling thistle heads. The goldfinches fed at the source, eating as they foraged, so the thistle down accumulated around the bases of the stems, chaff from the seeds strewn about inside the flower heads. Sparrows were flying off with the seeds, leaving no chaff in the seed heads.

There were thousands of rodent tracks in the fog-dampened sand, revealing their predawn, full summer activity. Insect trails crisscrossed everywhere. The more we looked, the more we found. We had to tear ourselves away from these stories, each one wanting to draw us in and hold us, to make progress toward the beach. Our excitement grew. We were caught up in the intense rush that tracking produces. We were diving into a deep pool. Sometimes it is best to forget the goals and just go with what presents itself.

Well, two and a half hours later, we finally managed to get within view of the ocean.

Time was passing fast, but we were nearing the creek mouth.

After a brief lunch, we headed once again toward the beach, but quickly got diverted in the foredunes by a busy world of intersecting tracks and multiple signs: mice, crows, skunks, sparrows, hawks and owls, rabbits, raccoons, buzzards, bobcat, gray fox, with cascades of new observations and questions. Tracks, scrapes, digs, bones, feathers, scat, urine marks and chews covered the landscape and demanded our attention. We hit a day of intense animal activity.

It wasn't until the last few minutes of the allotted class time that we finally made it to the shoreline, with barely enough time left for a closing circle and expressions of gratitude to the Earth and each other. I think of that day each time I get caught in haste and schedules. The tracker mind says to slow down and make each step one of wonder and curiosity. Watch how life then comes to meet you, revealing surprises at every turn, filling each moment with delight. Watch how clear your mind becomes and how easily answers fall into place.

There will always be deadlines and the impatience to meet them. But just as surely, we can notice the tension and make a shift, with a simple breath, back into presence. Awareness says to slow down and notice what comes along. Link the pieces together. It becomes a lively, unfolding story.

There is a kindness in the world of nature. Unlike the disoriented world of modern humanity, where we mistake *goal achieving* for *living*, nature will not slam the door in our face if we aren't quick enough or smart enough, if we don't fight for what we need. Instead, it opens its door willingly and generously. It invites us in and makes us welcome, reminding us that this was our original home, that there is nowhere else to get to.

The trick is to do both: let our physical mind do what it does best, making plans and getting carried away with hopes and dreams, while using our spiritual mind the way it is designed, for being alive in the present moment, in a state of courageous kindness and generosity, in a state of appreciative awareness. And I used to think it was just a walk to the beach!

July 2009

Invisibility

An essential skill in tracking, in any effort to get closer to nature, is the ability to become invisible. It is a skill that can be used to our advantage in many endeavors in daily life; you may already have a little practice.

The ability to set one's ego aside and participate in any activity in a whole-hearted, generous way is an aspect of invisibility. Teaching, at least in the coyote style, is a matter of getting out of the way and guiding a student to discoveries without your methods being obvious. Good parenting works in a similar manner—you want your child to grow into herself and learn in her own way so she will be flexible and responsive on her own. It is a widely applicable principle. Invisibility is a profound experience and an extremely illuminating practice.

In nature, becoming invisible means disappearing for all practical purposes. You are not, of course, actually invisible, but as far as animals are concerned, you are not there. It reminds me of one of my favorite passages from the Tao: "One does less and less until one does nothing at all, and when one does nothing at all there is nothing that is left undone." It is all about the meaning of "doing." In nature, nothing needs to be done. There is perfection in it, just as it is.

Invisibility uses the concepts of bird language and concentric rings. Essentially it is the practice of quieting your inner energy and movements until you are in such a state of harmony with the surroundings that you create no disturbances (concentric rings) in the local alarm systems (bird language). Birds are sometimes called the "voice of the forests" because they are so heavily invested in using calls and body language to communicate with each other about potential dangers nearby. Disturbances, such as a hunting predator or an oblivious human, will set off waves of alarm that spread in radiating circles across the landscape. Animals are aware of these rings of disturbance and know how to read them. It is a critical part of their survival.

We can begin to practice invisibility in nature by slowing down, breathing rhythmically, and moving quietly. Slowing ourselves down like this, opening our senses into acute awareness and becoming a part of the landscape, we move into a different state of mind. We shift from our thinking mind to our spiritual mind and follow our hearts rather than our thoughts. We slip into the landscape, instead of barging through in a loud clatter. Our own footsteps begin to sound unpleasantly loud, and we instinctively step more lightly. We can experience this state of inner silence anywhere, whether we are hiking down the middle of a dirt road, scrambling through huckleberry thickets in the woods, or just walking across the yard.

When we relax, step more quietly, and move more harmoniously with the sounds in nature, using them to mask the sounds of our own movement, we shift into invisibility. Like erasing a blackboard, our profile fades out and disappears. This is when good things begin to happen. While it is easiest to do this alone, it is rewarding to develop a close enough relationship with a friend to do it as a team.

One day, when I first began learning about these skills, I went for a walk in the forest up on the ridge. It was late afternoon, and the usual summer winds were blowing briskly through the woods. I was strolling along quietly, came around a corner, and there, only about thirty feet away, was a bobcat sitting in the middle of the trail. I stopped instantly, but the bobcat saw me and ran off into the woods. Thinking about these concepts of invisibility, I decided to see if I could find the cat. I triangulated and cut a path through the trees toward where I thought the cat might have gone. I moved very, very slowly, using the gusts of wind to mask the sounds of my footsteps in the forest debris. I shifted into a state of heightened awareness while simultaneously calming myself, slowing my breathing and heart rate. I drifted with the winds, becoming a shadow, slipping silently through the brush.

About forty feet into the forest, I realized that I had become so totally absorbed in my effort to be silent that I had momentarily stopped looking around. I lifted my gaze and scanned ahead and started! There, only ten feet away, was the bobcat, sitting next to a tree trunk, staring at me. He was just where I thought he would be. My silence had worked. He had only gone a short way and was simply waiting for me to clear the area before going back to his business.

Tom Brown always said that wild animals enjoy being talked to, that it makes them relax and feel curious, so I started talking in a low voice to this bobcat, making up stories, telling him how much I like cats, telling him all about my own cat, making small talk but with a feeling of caring. He stared at me, cocked his head a little, listened, and didn't move. I continued talking in a calm voice, while avoiding looking directly into his eyes.

I decided to push it. While still talking, I took a few more very slow, quiet, indirect steps toward him, just to see how close he'd allow me. I stopped at about five feet. It seemed enough. My heart was pounding, though my outside demeanor was still. The bobcat looked at me one last time, curious, perhaps confused, and then in a relaxed and fluid motion, stood up, turned and disappeared into the thickets. The theory of invisibility had just become much more real.

How and when we move makes all the difference. You can mask your presence and pull in those rings of alarm that you send across the landscape by knowing how to avoid sparking disturbances in bird communities around you. And conversely, with knowledge of the songs and calls of the common birds who occupy an area, and a sense of the meaning of their often subtle movements, you can tell when they are beginning to get nervous, but before they have sent out the alarm. At the same time, they can tell you a great deal about what is going on beyond your own sensory sphere.

The Apache scouts were probably the world's greatest masters of these skills. They honed the art of invisibility to its highest perfection. Stories of Apaches suddenly appearing out of nowhere are a movie cliché: the inscrutable Indian somehow crosses the uncrossable river and appears in the middle of the town without anyone having noticed his approach; Geronimo making good on his threat, slipping through the fortifications in the middle of the night to leave his knife stuck through the cavalry general's hat on his bedside table. There is an air of mystery to those stories, but the mysticism is practical. It's not really a mystery at all. It is a way of being.

These stories are rooted in two things. It was the scout's job to remain on the edges of his territory, living invisibly for extended periods of time, setting off no alarms while at the same time being acutely aware of the presence of any potential enemy, whose skills were equally advanced. These scouts could read the landscape for miles around. It was the ultimate cat and mouse game. They knew how to identify blind spots and hide in them. They knew how to move under the mask of other sounds and movement, and in the shadows between bright spots. These people were deeply connected to their own landscape, just as we can be to our own.

At the same time, almost any hunter-gatherer had a profoundly different concept of his relationship to nature and even his sense of "self" as a separate entity. There is certainly a spiritual aspect to it, in that one can shift into the "force" or the "Tao," into the place where all things are connected, and essentially disappear. But it is a skill that runs in a continuum, and anyone who is willing to give it a try can experience it. Certainly with practice, knowledge, and dedication, the skill grows. But it doesn't take much to start: go outside, pay attention to how you feel, calm down, and see what happens. Learn as you go. Learn from each step. Nature is there to be stepped into. Nature constantly offers this gift, and it is well worth taking.

March 2010

Mrs. Bobcat

Not too long ago, I met a beautiful animal who I've been trying to track down for the last several months. In a place I frequent around Limantour Beach, though I shouldn't reveal exactly where out of respect for her, I began to notice her tracks showing up consistently. It had to be a regular pattern, so I decided to see if I could meet her. I followed her trails many times. It was clear that this was one of her favorite areas and that she came here often.

I tried to learn who she was from those tracks—how she moved, where she went, where she stopped, what she did. It reminded me of something Tom Brown once said at one of his classes: that tracking can be an invasion of privacy, because it is such an intimate view into who someone is. In tracks, nothing can really be hidden. In fact, reading the tracks of an animal or a human can actually reveal much more than watching them moving.

So, I followed her tracks, over and over, while still being careful to respect her privacy and avoid any sense of violating spiritual boundaries. But over time, I did feel that I was getting to know her and was, in a way, beginning to build a relationship.

Her tracks were very round, with no obvious toenails, with strides about twenty inches long. The ridge between the ball of her foot and her toes formed a nice C-shaped arc. She often walked in an overstep, back foot stepping beyond front foot, yet the tracks were usually in a steady walking gait. The rear footprints were often spaced a little wider than the front footprints. Each track was about one and three quarters of an inch in diameter and seemed to have been set very carefully and flat footed, without much slapping or blowout around the tracks—she walked with a steady and light-footed gait. This track was adding up to a female bobcat.

Sometimes, the tracks from several journeys back and forth were visible, each one more aged than the next, a pattern that fit with a bobcat's hunting routine. I backtracked and found that they often emerged from a thicket of willows in a wind-protected gulch. The trail into the thicket was marked by many scats, some old and white, some fresh and dark, with the dense, segmented, tootsie-roll shape typical of bobcat scat. The scats were composed mostly of the tightly compacted fine grey fur of mice and voles, with occasional concentrations of the longer soft brown fur of brush rabbits, but sometimes they were full of grey feather remnants from coots. I could find bits of bones and small vole jaws in the scat, so I knew she traveled to the grassy fields a short distance away.

The trails leading out of the gulch branched in three directions, a pattern called a feeding manifold: one uphill into brush, one along the shoreline of a pond towards chaparral-covered slopes, and the third in between, toward a grassy bluff. There were occasional accumulations of scats quite a distance from the thicket, marking smaller side runs cutting off toward hunting areas. Careful measurement showed a close similarity between the scat at the hunting spots and the scat near the thicket. The picture emerging was of a sheltered resting spot connected to a variety of hunting areas marked off as the cat's territory, with a stable daily routine typical of a female bobcat.

It looked like the tracks were made both in the evenings and mornings, possibly in response to patterns of small prey animal activities that in turn reflected the changing local winds, temperatures, and moonlight. Sometimes the gait would speed up briefly from the walk into a trot and then into a lope. It was fun to become the cat, to slip into her spirit while following its tracks and sense how it might have felt at these spots, perhaps a little too exposed, with a need to hurry home. I could see the precise steps where the speed-ups and slow-downs occurred, right at the most open areas.

I became determined to see her. I went out before dawn a few times, hid in the brush below the thickets where I had a good view of her regular route, and waited to see the cat in action. No dice. Frustrating. So I decided to try dusk instead, and went out on a warm summer evening.

I took up a position above the thicket this time, on the route to the brushy hillside. I found a little wrinkle in the land where I'd be somewhat hidden. I lay down, settled in, and shifted to a patient, timeless state of awareness. The sun had just set, the sand was warm, and the wind had died. A profound quiet settled on the land. I was scanning the bobcat's manifold zone when I noticed a skunk ambling along in my direction in that typically unconcerned way they have, its startling black and white stripes immediately drawing my attention. It was trundling along a few feet away from the regular route of the bobcat, just outside of a line of brush.

I did a double take and saw that, paralleling it on the opposite side of the brush, was the bobcat. The skunk looked absorbed in its own thoughts and plans, but the cat was curious and kept apace, peeking at the skunk in between bushes, until the skunk suddenly tired of the game—not as oblivious as it appeared—and abruptly came around and stopped to confront the cat. Nose to nose they froze in a direct stare-down, the skunk vibrating its tail threateningly and fluffing its fur out to appear as big as possible.

The cat held her position for a moment but quickly became intimidated and began to disengage, turning her head slowly and backing away, one very careful step at a time, while the skunk held its ground (probably with a very angry look on its face). Once she had backed three or four feet away, the cat relaxed a little, turned, and moved more quickly till she was about ten feet away, then sat down to watch the skunk out of the corner of her eye, from a safer distance.

She yawned, looked away and licked a paw as if quite unconcerned, conceding the moment to the skunk and giving it time to move along. The skunk, having made it quite clear who was boss, dropped its tail, turned, and resumed its beautiful little undulating lope. The bobcat sat where it was, well hidden in the brush, reviewing what had just happened, licking its paws in a show of nonchalance, as we both watched the skunk continue on its way.

I looked back toward the bobcat. In the blink of an eye, in the gathering dusk, she was gone. Since then, I've managed to see her a couple more times. I hope to eventually have a conversation, but I'm trying to move slowly with her, building up trust over a period of time. I don't want to spook her by imposing myself too quickly. I want to give her a chance to become curious about me. She is a wild animal, and that is sacred. I wouldn't want to change that. Yet perhaps a healthy friendship, a mutual recognition, is possible.

March 2015

Close to Skunks

I have a great affection for skunks. With that wonderful banner-like tail waving behind, our common striped skunk ripples across the land like wind blowing across a grassy slope. Up close, they have amazingly cute little face with intense, inquisitive eyes and very active noses, incessantly sniffing everything around them. A narrow white stripe runs from the black nose tip to the white cap between their small black ears. They are really quite endearing. But it was only when I started tracking skunks that I began to truly understand and appreciate them.

Skunks are evening foragers, most commonly seen at dusk. They seem to appear out of nowhere, quite absorbed in their tasks, rummaging relentlessly across the landscape. Though they seem happiest and most at home weaving and foraging through dense thickets, in open country, such as the meadows on Mount Wittenberg or the dunes out at Limantour, they will often go on long journeys across the expanses, traveling along in a steady lope, with little fear of predation, clearly with destinations in mind.

Their baseline lope, a comfortable "rocking horse" gait, with the tail waving in turn, is responsible for their rippling motion. In sand, the tracks often run in a long series of short diagonal lines, four prints in little groups about eight inches long, known as a transverse lope or sometimes called a slant-four. On open sand, you will often see these diagonal lines steadily meandering off into the distance.

The front feet of skunks have long, well-developed digging claws that register as part of the track and fused metacarpal pads that amplify their digging power. I have followed their trails many times, watching the tracks age and begin to disappear as the sun dries them out and the wind breaks them down. Finally, all that will be left are the four small puncture marks from their claws, still identifiable by the size, pattern, and stride. When they are hunting for insects around shrubs and along trails, they will often leave numerous little cone-shaped digs, a primary sign of their presence. In winter, in particular, they will hunt for beetles and other large insects who have taken shelter in shallow ground burrows under the protective layers of old dry grasses. Their foraging will leave a grassy slope covered with circular holes in the old grass layer, looking almost woven like bird nests because of how they part the grasses before they start digging.

Like many animals who defend themselves with poison, skunks have remarkably bold coloration, which serves as an obvious warning to other animals (including us) so they are not forced to use their weapon unnecessarily. This is similar to the credo of the Apache Scout, as reported by Tom Brown in his discussions of his mentor's warrior philosophy. It is said that the last thing the true warrior wants to do is pick up his lance, with which he can easily kill, knowing that even his enemy is a brother. He also knows that once weapons are drawn, injury to oneself is all too likely; peace is always the best choice. The skunk similarly seems leery of conflict, but quite confident in his weaponry and his reputation. This was clearly illustrated by a recent close encounter I had.

I was lying in a wrinkle of land at dusk, quietly observing the progress of a skunk who was heading out for its evening forage, loping along in its self-absorbed, unconcerned way. It looked like he was going to pass just below, but suddenly he turned and headed directly toward me, heedless of my presence, showing the remarkable lack of worry, or even awareness, which a skunk can afford.

I was lying very still. I didn't want to startle him and hoped he would see me, but he kept on coming. Now, I'm not particularly worried about skunks. I know they are reluctant to spray (though very accurate when they do) because it is their last resort weapon, and an extremely effective one at that. But as he got closer, I realized he was completely unaware of me and I began to worry about surprising him, so at the last minute, when he was two or three feet from my outstretched legs, I wiggled my foot just a little to catch his attention. It worked. He was shocked! His reverie shattered, he looked at me with wide angry eyes, his tail immediately going up, hair standing on end and vibrating.

Then followed one of the more amazing things I've ever seen an animal do. In a series of moves, he made a feint at me, a four-legged lunge forward, followed by three or four lurches backward, then another short lunge forward and another series of backward lurches, until, facing me the whole time, he had backed up fifteen feet. The tracks were simply two parallel grooves, which would have been very difficult to interpret, had I not just seen them made. At that point, the little skunk simply turned along the original trajectory and continued on his way in that same myopic, wobbly little lope, as if the encounter had never happened!

The whole incident illustrated something I have seen over and over again in my wanderings. Animals can show a lot of curiosity, fear, respect, and competitiveness toward each other. But except when the hunt is actually on, they also show a great deal of tolerance, even between predator and prey, and seem very reluctant to become aggressive.

When I first started to practice the principles of silent stalking and tracking, I began having startling close-up experiences with animals. From face-to-face encounters with sharp-antlered bucks I was tracking through the forests, to a close-up "hello!" with a cougar south of Arch Rock one evening, and even once swimming quietly into a group of feeding pelicans who then thoroughly intimidated me with their size and long sharp bills, these kinds of meetings were unnerving at first. I could sense the primal, unpredictable energy in the animals, especially the ones with tooth, claw, bill, or antler. It was amazing how easy it was, with the right skills, to move in amongst animals in a way I never had before. It could be a little scary to come face to face with a powerful wild creature, unsure what its next move might be, afraid I'd violated a boundary and might be attacked.

Over time though, I have learned that this is not how nature works. If we move with gentleness and calmness, and a little respect, most animals will allow us to come inside the usual caution zone. I keep getting the feeling that they are curious about us, and would like to get to know us better if we weren't so darn loud and unaware, violating the basic rules. If we were a little calmer, they'd probably like to invite us right into their living rooms for a good conversation.

May 2009

Schooner Bay

Here in Point Reyes, there was a dramatic and polarizing controversy some years ago about whether or not to close the old oyster farm in Drakes Estero, one of the few designated marine wilderness areas in the nation. In the end, after a great deal of local pressure to keep the farm open, the Department of the Interior decided that a commercial business was incompatible with wilderness and closed the farm. As a quiet supporter of the idea of a naturalized estero without commercial operations, I am pleased with the outcome. I'm sorry so many people ended up disappointed, but in terms of world treasures, Drakes Estero is one of the greatest. It is a miracle to have the Point Reyes Peninsula as intact as it is. It is well worth protecting. The next move is to work on protecting it from our own recreational overuse.

To that end, I advocate being in nature as undisruptively as possible. But be in it! I believe that intimate knowledge of your home territory, whether you are migratory and dispersed—a tourist—or a year-round resident, gives one a stake in what happens there. When we have a stake in it, we go beyond being mere stewards of the land to actually owning it. Once we are a part of it, it is ours: now it matters what junk I leave behind! Now it matters what waters I pollute, what habitats and ecosystems I damage. If it is home, I can't so easily overlook my own sloppy treatment of it.

So, since I now feel more ownership of Schooner Bay and its surrounding bluffs, I decided it would be a good idea to track the area and establish a good baseline, to get to know it better from a tracker's standpoint. I'd do a transect, a wander, sort of size it up. For all of my years of hiking and exploring around Point Reyes, I had never set foot in that little back corner of this mighty wetland. So off I went early one morning, to walk a circle on the bluffs between the old oyster operation in Schooner Bay and the wing of the estero to the south, Home Bay.

The very name of this bay is amazing. After the establishment of ranches in the 1800s, commodities were shipped to San Francisco by boat, in or out of these remote shallow bays. I wonder what the depths of the waters were then, compared to now, to allow those small ships so far into the interior ranch lands, and how they negotiated the treacherous channels to get in and out.

The prior occupants of the area, the Miwoks, may not have appreciated the romantic ring of the name Schooner Bay; they probably had older names and built livelihoods around the bivalve harvest, lasting for thousands of years before overharvest by the newcomers quickly exhausted the ancient beds.

A stroll up and over the hill is very familiar and comfortable to me. It is classic Marin coastland, the kind of landscape I grew up in. The canyons and slopes can be brambly thickets, while the bluff-tops are open, having been intentionally kept that way, by burning, since Neolithic times. Cows graze it heavily now, so the fields of annual grasses are cropped low, and the coyote brush is small and thinly spaced. Wild iris fields, lavender to deep purple, immune to the cattle, stretched brilliantly across the slopes for acres.

Out here, gopher is king. The soil, derived from ancient seabed substrates, is forgiving and drains well, and the plant community that survives the cattle grazing tends toward tuberous roots that work well for the gopher, especially in late dry season. Current gopher tailings are everywhere. On the other hand, voles, a primary food for every predator around, are infrequent across these grazed lands because they need tall layers of old grasses to hide their half-tunnel surface runs.

The canyons are throwing out a symphony of birdcalls from all the lovely locals: quail, flicker, towhee, scrub jay, wrentit, golden crown, and white crown sparrow. The foliage in the thickets includes all the regulars: twinberry, blackberry, stinging and hedge nettles, hemlock and cow parsnip, wild cucumber, poison oak. The canyon bottoms host red and yellow willows, rushes and cattails, coffee berry trees, a few big old cypress trees, a smattering of pine. The meadows are covered with annual grasses, sheep sorrel, plantain, paintbrush, soap root, thistles, geranium, pimpernel, yarrow, dandelion, blue-eyed grass—all the familiar faces. On the more ocean-facing slopes, mugwort and bracken ferns appear in the thickets.

Along the cattle trails on the side slopes and the old ranch roads on the bluffs, there is a steady spacing of bobcat scats, mostly containing gopher fur and bones, sometimes including the impressively large gopher incisor teeth, dark orange from the concentration of iron that hardens them for digging. Occasional brush rabbit fur and foot bones show up in the scat, and there are duck and coot feathers in the scats near the ponds. Finally, as I move beyond the grazing meadows to side hills of thick and heavy grasses, little vole runs appear like lights turning on, here, there, then everywhere. Close inspection reveals their tiny scat in the nicely mown "porches" at the edges of bramble thickets, and the bobcat scats down here contain little vole jaws.

More birds as I move along: the raven pairs clucking to each other as they fly over, crow and scrub jay calling raucously. The red-tailed hawks and turkey vultures gliding overhead. Requisite mallard pairs at each cattle pond. Occasional cormorants and Caspian terns—the fishermen—flying, croaking, over the bluff from one bay to another. Redwing blackbirds calling and singing around the ponds, ruffing their neon red epaulets, cliff swallows swooping along the margins. Red and blue dragonflies. A three-inch leopard frog.

There was a brush fire through the first canyon some years ago that cleared a lot of tall coyote brush and stimulated an invasion of

Scotch broom. Invasives must be considered on a species by species basis, but Scotch broom is, in my view and the view of park ecologists, a serious pest, spreading quickly and choking out native plants. I come upon some park employees who are working on this patch, hand clearing close to the bay, but using herbicides further from the water. At this point I'm okay with minimal use of herbicides. I'm still doing my own research on the hazards of Roundup, but in the meantime, I trust the botanists and ecologists. The cost effectiveness comparison of herbicides versus manual labor, in the battle against aggressive invasive plants, is compelling.

Coyote scat is virtually absent out here. I'm surprised at this, given the larder of gophers, but Schooner Bay is close to Abbotts Lagoon, a short trot for a coyote. The Abbotts coyotes, which I've tracked for years, travel overland to the shores of the estero. Abbotts has undergone an almost complete collapse of its jackrabbit population in the last three years, and coyotes have all but vacated the area. It seems to have become a marginal territory now, occupied by unaffiliated loners, mouse hunters. On the other hand, the coyote family that I'm familiar with further inland, near Point Reyes Station, is still strong, singing most evenings, and I often see jackrabbits there late at night and just before dawn.

Raccoons, the wet-edge foragers, leave tracks at every muddy shoreline. Deer sign is strangely infrequent right now, but finally on the bluff top, I find clusters of their pellets. Nearby, and spread across the high areas, are multiple shallow-angle badger digs—they must just love this gopher country! The occasional straight-down single holes, more likely dug by coyotes, give an indication that coyotes occasionally swing through on gopher patrol.

I could have kept on like this for days, peering into the ecology of these coastal bluffs, but for now it was enough. I had a pretty good idea of the patterns of life out here. A sweet land in quiet repose. The former oyster company site looks clean and pristine, at least from a superficial view. Nature feels balanced and safe. It feels like home.

July 2015

Birds of a Feather

Among the most remarkable creations in nature is the bird feather. Its refinements boggle the mind in their complexity. The feather is one of the most durable and long-lasting structures in animal life; it is a miracle of bioengineering, a mix of strength, lightness, and insulation, while enabling a wide range of flight styles in nearly all environments. For a tracker, feathers are an important part of the information nature has to offer. It does not take long to learn how to read the shapes of feathers to tell what part of a bird they came from, and once the various classes of coloration patterns start to register in our minds, and a sense of context and habitat is applied, identifying a bird by a single feather becomes more and more possible.

A feathered wing makes flight possible because of its air-foil effect: The curved shape of the top forces air to speed up, spreading out the molecules and creating slightly lower air pressure on the top compared to the bottom. This gives the bird lift, as the wing wants to rise to adjust to the pressure difference. Through this simple but utterly profound principle, animal evolution found a way to make flight become a reality.

Birds have an amazing spectrum of wing shapes and flight styles, from albatrosses, with their slender, twelve-foot wingspan designed for gliding thousands of miles over windy oceans, to the unassuming wrentit, with its short, rounded wings designed for flitting through brush in a territory smaller than an acre. The wrentit, and most passerines (small perching birds), fly with an undulating burst of flapping to gain speed and altitude, followed by a glide with wings outstretched. A similar style is the bounding flight of the woodpecker, who alternates bursts of flapping with glides in which its wings fold back against its body.

Ducks come sweeping fast into ponds and marshes like little fighter squadrons; their slender, boomerang-shaped, high-speed wings enable a constant, powered flight style. Other high-speed birds, such as falcons and swallows, use the same wing shape to achieve both high velocity and extreme agility. Quite opposite is the "thermal soaring" of eagles, red-tailed hawks, and vultures, who employ broad wings and rising air masses to gain lift. In between these forms is the elliptical-shaped wing of game birds, short and broad with deep slotting in the wingtips. This shape allows for the noisy, startling, high-acceleration burst when they flush from the ground, an important defense against ground predators. But for all the flight styles and wing shapes, flight feathers are remarkably similar across species. The primary wing feather of a hummingbird has essentially the same structure as that of an eagle one thousand times its weight!

I was thinking of these things on a recent walk near the coast when a turkey vulture flew over at a low altitude; it circled and caught an up-running wave in the onshore breeze caused by the small hill where I stood. The bird circled several times overhead, and I could see it adjusting its wing tips; when it came into the breeze and slowed down, losing lift, it spread its primary feathers so slots appeared in the outer six to eight inches of the wingtips, giving it that familiar fingery look. But when it circled around and flew downwind, it closed the slots as it sped up and gained lift. The buzzard did this each time it circled, and with each circle it rose higher until it had reached a sufficient height to release itself from the elevator and soar out over the fields further downwind.

Turkey vultures, and other soaring birds, have cutaways on the trailing edges of their long primary feathers. With precise control, they can spread their wingtips to create slots between the feathers. As the wind rushes through the narrow channels of the slots, the bird gains additional lift. When we look up high and see a red-tailed hawk flying in lazy circles as it rides a thermal bulge, both its wings and wing slots are stretched as wide as possible. This, along with the hawk's broad, high-lift wing shape, enables extremely slow flight in the search for prey.

While primary wing feathers are responsible for speed and control, secondary wing feathers—shorter, more rounded at the tips, and more symmetrical—are responsible for most of the wing's shape and lift. There is also a sophisticated array of other types of feathers over the wings and body of a bird: The most obvious are the coverlets, which smooth and shape the wings and body, and the rudders, the specialized and highly controllable tail feathers. Beneath the coverlets is an uneven layer of down feathers, the ultimate insulator, and two types of sensory feathers, plumes and quills, which work much like a mammal's guard hairs and whiskers, giving the bird a high level of body awareness.

The dizzying array of colors and patterns on feathers ranges from the perfect cryptic camouflage of ground-feeders, such as quail and grouse, to the obvious and colorful patterns on birds that take to the trees. It was just this move into the safety of trees, made possible by flight and evoked by the tree, that afforded the possibility of showy color patterns. I'm always amazed at the complex patterns that can found in each feather. Birds achieve these colors in a variety of ways. Melanin pigments, responsible for blacks, greys, and browns, and porphyrin pigments, responsible for pinks, light browns, and greens, are manufactured in the bird's body. But carotenoids, which create the bright reds and yellows that are particularly prominent in courting displays, notably the redwinged blackbird, must be ingested from plants.

Blue colors are not pigments at all; known as "structural" colors, they result from refractive qualities in the feather itself.

Many species, especially among the high-speed birds such as gulls, utilize the fact that wingtips wear out over the course of a year, creating different patterns as the seasons change. The melanin in black portions of a feather is harder and wears out more slowly than white portions. White feather tips are bright and obvious in the new mating plumage in spring, but as these tips wear out and high visibility no longer serves its important purpose, the bird becomes darker and more cryptic. The opposite is true as well—many songbirds develop their breeding plumage by the darker edges of their winter feathers wearing away and revealing the more colorful spring patterns.

There are highly variable patterns of molting too, through which brightly colored breeding plumage changes into the subdued colors more appropriate to nesting. Many birds molt once a year, and some have another partial molt just before breeding season. Migratory birds often molt twice during the year, once before the migration, in the summer, and once before breeding. It takes a lot of precious energy to grow a new set of feathers, so the economy is to take care of this in between the high-energy months of nesting or traveling. I like to call late summer the "feather-finding" season, for it is when the raptors are replacing their big primary feathers. To maintain flight balance, they shed the same feather on each wing, in a progression from tip on down, so if you look up at a vulture or hawk at that time of year, you might notice a gap on each side.

I never fail to be amazed at the beauty and complexity, and the infinite palette of the colors and patterns, on feathers, and even more how those individual feather patterns add up to entirely different patterns when overlapped over the whole bird. Even more, birds purposefully alter their colors and patterns by how they spread their wings and fan their tails, revealing how deeply evolved these colors and patterns are, a language among birds as important as their calls and songs. And we can be assured that if these patterns are so infinitely varied and complex, avian vision is correspondingly astute.

Just as the thickets evoked the life form of the bobcat, and the open hills called forth the coyote, the air itself created flight and birds, and the release from gravity led to the tremendous beauty of infinitely varied color patterns. The physics of the air contained the possibility of flight; life responded with an ever-refining process of adaptation and change. The earth, its plants and its birds, and we ourselves continue to co-evolve in this ongoing dance. It does not fail to bring a smile to my heart when I realize that the beautiful spotted towhee flitting through my trees is carrying an echo of a past that reaches back hundreds of millions of years.

April 2017

Summer Stories

Early summer in the wild parts of West Marin is always a time of mystery and surprise, and this year, in the drought, even more so. In my casual observations, it has been striking how quickly and dramatically the signs of our major predators, the bobcat and coyote, have diminished around hiking trails. Reports from tracker friends in surrounding areas indicate similar patterns. What is going on here? How is the current down cycle in the populations of our major prey species, the vole and brush rabbit, related to this deviation? The land begs for answers to these fundamental questions. Meanwhile, and contrarily, the gopher population is booming throughout the area, but is that enough to compensate? To me, as a tracker, the intrigue is stimulating.

With these changes and drop-offs in apparent animal presence, I am more thrilled than ever to see any signs of predator activity in my favorite tracking areas, and I eagerly scrutinize the smallest details for indications of the pulse of life and the moods running through the invisible animal world. So I was gratified to come upon a single coyote trail near the beach the other day.

I was leading a small family on a private tracking walk. It had been a fine adventure, but the younger kids were starting to tire out and get distracted. Feeding signs were subtle, scats were old (though still yielding information), and tracks were scarce. I had dusted out a section of trail the previous evening at a spot which usually collects a fine array of tracks overnight—skunks loping through on their evening forages, bobcats occasionally walking by on their way to rodent-rich thickets, coyotes trotting in their never-ending quests, deer families browsing along the trail edges, brush rabbits playing and nibbling, mice and even shrews crisscrossing in various bound patterns, sparrows hopping and skipping across while foraging for night-dropped seeds. But it was nearly bare that morning.

For a day like this, I was surprised. None of the expected activity appeared in the fine dust. We found just one mouse track and one beautiful beetle trail, clearly registering the differences between front, middle, and back feet. But this was not the kind of tracking that readily engages the imagination of young neophyte trackers. We continued on to the dunes.

The sand at the coast is very dry and loose at this time of year, and our late start did not afford us the use of the dawn-fog dampness for track clarity. By mid-morning the sun and wind had broken all detail down, but the beauty of summer sand is how it can teach us to use size, scale, pattern, and context for track interpretation. Without recourse to textbook-clear tracks with sharp pad and toe details, a tracker is forced to step back a little and observe the gaits and overall shapes of tracks, to wonder who would have been moving across the landscape at this particular spot, to imagine the size of the animal from the length of the strides and how it moved. It is good practice in visualizing the animal, trying to picture it as if it was coming to life right there in front of you. Still, for the kids, it was a stretch.

So it was a delight, and relief, to find a fresh trail crossing over the top of all the older craters and contours in the dry sand. Even in this dry substrate, the edges of the new tracks were obviously sharper and more detailed than the surrounding tracks, and the splashes of sand around the edges were still slightly off-color. The size of the tracks—about three inches long—the oval shape, the slight hints of heel pad and toenails, the stride length, and even the way it had meandered into this location all quickly told me this was a coyote trail. The long S-shaped arcs in the incoming trail perfectly characterized coyote movement, mimicking the shifting breezes.

The overstep pattern—smaller rear foot landing in front of the larger front foot with each step—along with the relatively short stride length and widening straddle told me this coyote had slowed down here, either moving comfortably in an unhurried, foraging, inspecting state of mind or perhaps, hearing something out of baseline, stepping carefully, senses alert. It was hard to say, given the lack of detail, but something in the whole scenario gave me the feeling that this coyote had been very relaxed when it crossed by here. It looked recent, mid-day, so perhaps it had finished hunting for the morning and was heading somewhere to take a nap.

The trail went forward ahead of us, then took a sharp turn to the left, went straight for about fifteen feet, then turned abruptly to the right, where the coyote had suddenly taken off in a fast lope and the trail disappeared into the dunes. Assessing all of this, we began to look more closely and found a series of unusual drag marks, each about a foot long, along the straight section of this trail, before it turned right and took off.

My first thought was that the coyote had playfully picked up a stick, carried and dragged it a ways, then dropped it and ran off. That would have been interesting enough, but there was no stick. When I got down to look more closely, I could see that the drag marks were in a rhythmic pattern that was unrelated to the strides of the coyote. Curiosity piqued and looking yet more closely, I found a series of three-inch, K-shaped tracks in between each set of drag marks—the classic track of a great horned owl, who may have been foraging for insects during the moonlit night. The drags were from its long rear talons. These owls have a tendency to walk in very straight lines with abrupt direction changes when they are hunting on the ground. I don't know why, but perhaps they are navigating by sound, even when walking, going straight to their slow-moving prey, in this instance probably beetles.

Using pressure release and aging analysis, I could see that the coyote had come upon the owl trail much later, perhaps on mid-morning patrol, and, by smell or sight—an interesting question in itself—it had turned and followed the owl trail to the point where the owl had taken off in flight, leaving the classic dead-end trail of a bird. Once in a while, sand that was pushed aside by the pressure of the coyote's foot had spilled over into one of the owl tracks, a sure sign that the coyote had come by after the owl.

Aging was in agreement, the coyote's tracks having degraded less than the owl tracks. Even in that loose sand, this was apparent with a close inspection. Where the owl had flown off in the night was precisely where the coyote had abruptly dashed off in a full zig-zagging run, as if to catch up to its original intention, perhaps that nap, after this unexpected diversion.

This story in the sand capped the day and woke the boys up, rekindling their wild imaginations, and it left us all feeling excited and fulfilled to have gotten a brief glimpse into the interwoven lives of our fellow animals. We turned to begin the trek back to the cars, ready to leave on this high note.

Perhaps we had been quieter than we realized, so absorbed in reading this tale in the sand. We stepped over the first rise and there in front of us, twenty feet away, was the coyote herself, heading right toward us in the early afternoon. She stopped in her tracks but didn't panic with the surprise. She looked right at us with those penetrating eyes, then turned and slowly walked away.

We all stood there in shock, amazed and surprised, yet still appreciating her exquisite beauty and feeling her great intelligence from the power of her gaze. We witnessed the way she assessed us, quickly came to her conclusions, and decided what to do. It was a perfect lesson. I gave thanks.

August 2012

Common Humanity and the Apache Scout

What is it that makes us truly human? What qualities represent the highest aspects of the human mind? Joseph Chilton Pearce, a twentieth century author who wrote about child development, did some thought-provoking work on these questions. He described three levels of our brain development—the "reptilian," the "mammalian," and the "human"—that reflect the evolutionary development of our brain from the core to the outer lobes. His work has shown that proper care and nurturing of a child is essential for higher brain development, particularly at critical stages in a child's growth, and that if this nurturing environment is missing or insufficient, brain development can be incomplete and very difficult to compensate in later life.

He pointed out that in the last century or two, in the era of industrialization and the unsustainable exploitation of human and natural resources, more and more children have been raised with inadequate nurturing in an increasingly hardened and traumatized world. This has been a culturally regressive process, leaving our higher capacities incompletely formed. Thus, we tend to confuse intellectual brilliance with higher humanity. Instead of using our human mind for its highest functions, such as caring, empathy, kindness, and tolerance, we have become more and more focused on so-called "achievements" such as miniaturizing nuclear bombs and executing billion-dollar corporate marketing campaigns. These are extremely complex tasks requiring a remarkable level of brilliance, amazing amounts of cooperation and almost unimaginable technical skills . . . yet they are insane.

We know there is something wrong with this, that something serious is lost along with all the gains. We may have longer and easier lives, but are they better? Perhaps we can look back to the roots of human consciousness, to ways of life that made us human, for answers. Anthropological reports consistently characterize older communities, the original hunter-gatherers, as being more gentle and nourishing with their children, and with each other, than modern "civilized" humans. Indigenous peoples, the Apaches in the American Southwest for example, may have achieved a true pinnacle of human development and culture, despite how unimpressive its material culture was compared to ours.

The Apache Scout, as Tom Brown describes it, was a warrior, a formidable foe if called to fight. Yet he considered it a defeat to be forced to pick up his weapon for combat. He saw no glory in taking the life of an enemy. In his view, the true warrior would find a way around conflict, a remarkably Buddhist attitude. His highest goal was simply to keep his people safe and well fed. To these ends, he was a master of observation and stealth, able to slip through the landscape like a ghost, using finely tuned survival skills while concealing his own presence, practicing the art of "counter-tracking."

Counter-tracking has to do with hiding signs of your own presence as you move through the land. It means leaving no tracks, or if you do, wiping them out in such a way that the wiping out is also not noticeable. It involves an acute awareness of concentric rings—how our movements, our noise, even our thoughts, have effects that spread out to the world around us, just as all of the actions around us are creating overlapping waves of their own that are spreading toward us from across the land. It means mastering the skill of controlling our disruptions until we can slip almost invisibly through the world while at the same time reading these rings to monitor the presence of others before they come into view.

It means gathering food from the land in such a way that the gathering is not noticeable. For example, twigs of an edible shrub can be cut so that the cuts are not only unnoticeable (to an enemy scout) but actually enhance the growth of the productive parts of the plant so it will provide more food in the future. It means making shelter in such a way that your shelter has very little impact on the land. It means harvesting materials to benefit the earth and increase the production of more materials. It means making a fire in such a way that very little fuel is burned and the remnants can be scattered in an instant. It is the ultimate form of sustainability.

Scouts would enhance abundance as they moved through the world, improving conditions for the benefit of future generations. This attitude leads directly to the idea of caretaking or wild tending, the original roots of agriculture, by which native peoples for thousands of years cared for the world around them, making sure that every action increased productivity and hence ease, rather than depleting and polluting it. This is higher human functioning.

Now, I don't mean to imply that there ever was complete perfection in this practice among indigenous peoples or in any human society. The course of humanity is very long and complex. But over those eons, before centralized agriculture and its hierarchical social organization and nature-conquering imperatives, each of us had direct hunter-gatherer ancestors who lived in a highly balanced culture of harmony with the earth. Each of us is a descendant of people whose way of life was increasingly fulfilling and nurturing—producing the classic ease, intelligence, graciousness, and generosity of undisturbed pre-agricultural societies, qualities the conquering "higher culture" was nearly blind to.

This orientation toward the earth, this higher functioning, can also teach us how to live around each other. We can relate to each other with an awareness similar to the Apache scout, caretaking and tending each other, treading softly, staying attuned to the concentric rings of our own actions and carefully reading the messages around us. We can make sure our presence is healthy for others. We have a responsibility to leave each other in better condition than when we first passed by, which is, to me, the very definition of humanity.

Let's ask ourselves: How human am I? What kind of wake have I left behind today? How have I treated my child? How have I treated my community? How am I treating the earth as I move through my life? It is transformative to walk softly in the woods and watch it come to life and reveal its secrets. Even more profound is to practice this around each other and watch what good can come.

August 2011

The Public Beach

John Muir famously pointed out that any time you pull on a thread in nature, you find that it is connected to the whole universe. That truth is nowhere more evident than in the prosaic dry sand of a public beach. There is a secret world of interwoven animal life at any wild beach, and it takes only a little effort to begin to see it. Next time you walk out to a coastline, Limantour Beach for instance, slow down for a moment and look at the sand as you cross the dunes and head down to the shore. Slow down and begin noticing the details on the sand surface.

The short walk from the car to the surf takes you through several distinct habitats merging from one to another, each with its own characteristic life systems. You pass through estuary, mudflat, chaparral, back dunes, foredunes, upper beach, foreshore, and tidal wash. A complete ecological system is laid out here, a complex world of plants, insects, worms, crustaceans, birds and mammals deeply woven into this underlying fabric.

Right there in front of you, as you walk onto the beach, slightly hidden amongst hundreds of human tracks, are dozens of animal tracks and trails, dozens of interlocking stories. During the night and early dawn, when people have gone home, wildness asserts itself, and a different world comes to life. Though the sand is loose and dry at this time of year, in summer, the whole surface has a thin top crust, created in the morning when the sun and wind dried out the night-dampened sand.

This crust is the key to tracking here: anything that steps on the dried crust during the day and evening leaves a thin broken crust-edge around the perimeter of the track and loose sand in the floor. But a track made at night when the sand is damp will harden in the morning, leaving a crust not only around the edges, but across the floor and sides of the track as well, so all the details are preserved. Getting a sense of when different trails were made brings the chronology of the scene to life. It's a little like looking at a starry sky with an understanding of the three-dimensionality of the universe. It is so much more than a flat surface, deeper and more elaborate, and, in fact, alive and changing.

With this in mind, walking through this cross section of habitats, you can begin to decipher a little of what has taken place during the night and over the last few days. You are likely to see the tracks of many birds who forage the bounty of the coast: crows, jays, buzzards, gulls, ducks, plovers, sandpipers, herons, sparrows, and flycatchers. You will probably see the tracks of several mammals: deer, skunk, fox, bobcat and coyote; families of raccoons, solitary opossums, brush rabbits by the dozens, mice by the hundreds. You'll see tracks and signs of insects: black beetles, burrowing beetles, box elders, several fly species, ants, and spiders. You will find tracks of crabs and even, if you are lucky, the tracks of living sand dollars at extreme low tide.

There is mechanical logic in this diversity. If we step back and look at the structure of the beach, we can see that the foreshore is created by the forces of tidal action. The high point of the summer beach corresponds to the highest level of wave wash. The beach drops down and flattens out as it extends into the ocean. Extreme high tides and storm waves breach the high berm and wash great amounts of seaweed, grasses, kelp, and algae, along with the carcasses of dead sea birds and mammals, over the top, to deposit them across the inner beach.

In the surf line, hidden in the sand, uncountable shrimps, crabs, and other crustaceans and invertebrates live on the constant wash of nutrients brought in by the waves. Behind the foreshore berm, across the inner beach, numerous flies and other insects live on decaying plant and animal matter. Further back, where the lightest sand particles are blown and deposited by the constant winds, the dunes rise up and hold fresh water aquifers that support the dune grasses, coyote brush, and lupines, which in turn create the basis for mouse and rabbit survival and draw in the carnivores who hunt them.

The beach is a smorgasbord, an extravagant feast. All of the opportunists are out. The ravens, with their long toenail drags, and the gulls and buzzards inspect any possible food source, from mole crabs to seal carcasses. The sandpipers are probing the water edges while the plovers are dashing across the upper beach picking flies and larvae, their probe holes riddling the edges of any clump of kelp where flies have laid their eggs. During the night on low tides, raccoons leave their hideouts in the dunes and lope or trot down to the shore to pick up crabs and carry them back to their hidden middens under the trees, in their unique walk, while the striped skunks and an occasional spotted skunk relentlessly forage the sand in their erratic little lopes, seeking beetles and their larvae.

Up in the dunes, mice have been busy all night, speckling the sand around the dune grass stalks with their little bounding trails. They will range ten or fifteen feet, but not much more, onto the open sands where they are taking a risk to harvest windblown seeds and nighttime bugs. Driftwood and other objects farther out on the open sand provide workable shelter from night-hunting owls and will be surrounded by swirls of mouse tracks. The owls will often march fifty to a hundred yards across the sand in search of prey, leaving long, straight trails.

Meanwhile, the larger predators—the coyote, bobcat, and fox—have been patrolling for brush rabbits and mice, leaving long trails sinuously winding through the foredunes, speaking eloquently of how the landscape plays the animal. Coyote trails in particular will show a great deal of slowing down, speeding up, and looking all around, the coyote alert to everything around it on the way up the beach, but on the return route, after a successful hunt, they will drop into a steady, unvaried side trot, just wanting to get home.

Each day is a new story, changing throughout the year. The beach is a manuscript to be read, a song just waiting to be sung. So put down the Frisbee and the cooler for a moment and look around. One track and a little observation will begin to unravel this universe. A mouse track in the dunes, then, is related to the grasses and flies, to the bobcat and owl, to the winds and tides, to the moon and the stars, and to yourself, all so eternal yet so fragile. Take a moment to absorb and appreciate this world and your place in it. Even this public beach is a wilderness.

April 2012

Opossums

There is an animal in our midst who is iconic in our stories and myths yet is almost universally disliked in common culture. There are many conflicting attitudes and opinions about it, yet very little real knowledge. It is one of the oldest mammals in North America, yet is usually thought of as an unintelligent bumbler, barely able to get out of its own way, just a varmint. It is an animal whose core survival strategy is to accomplish just that: to be overlooked. The Virginia opossum!

When I think of opossums, I picture them scuttling down suburban streets late on summer nights—they are mostly nocturnal and forage widely when it is warm—or showing up as an occasional visitor to my compost pile when I put my trail camera on it to see what's happening out there. It has always struck me how well the various animals schedule their visits to the compost pile in order to avoid confrontations, but I have caught glimpses of my local opossum facing off with a raccoon, using one of its best tools—that big grimace showing a long row of dangerous-looking teeth. It is definitely intimidating, which is exactly what the little fellow intends to accomplish.

Those teeth are one of the windows into who this animal actually is. Opossums have more teeth—fifty—than any other mammal: a full set incisors, the nibblers, at the front; large sharp prey-catching canines at the corners; several carnassial teeth, the slicers down the sides; and a row of molars, the grinders, at the back. The teeth reflect the extreme generalist diet of the opossum. They will eat just about anything edible: carrion, small mammals, reptiles and amphibians, birds and bird eggs, and a wide variety of plant foods—seeds, nuts, greens, fruits, and compost.

The opossum is a marsupial mammal, not a rodent, who arose from pre-marsupial ancestors in North and South America, about the time of the large dinosaur extinctions, seventy million years ago. I think of the marsupials as a transition animal, bridging the distance between the egg-laying reptiles and true live-birth mammals. It is truly an ancient animal form. They went extinct in North America after the continents separated, possibly because of ice ages they could not tolerate, but about three million years ago, when the continents reconnected, their South American relatives recolonized North America, where they adapted well to the hardwood sapling forests and brushy thickets of the American Southeast and Appalachia and became a staple of the southern diet, often cooked with sweet potatoes. The name itself, opossum, is taken from the Algonquin name for them that early colonists picked up, meaning "white rat."

Around 1910 they were introduced into California at San Jose, probably as a food source for stew-pot hunters, and they have spread widely in our state since, becoming nearly ubiquitous except in the coldest climates, limited by their bare ears and tail.

That tail is part of their mythical status. It is indeed prehensile, but the American opossum cannot actually hang from its tail as depicted in children's books. (There is an Australian species that can, which is how this got mixed up.) Our opossum uses its tail for balance and grip when climbing, and will gather leaves in a bunch and carry them with its tail when building one of its day beds, allowing it to use all four feet for climbing. And climb they do! Their feet have several specialized adaptations.

The opossum's distinctive tracks were one of the first things that really began to pique my curiosity about this animal. Though this animal looks rather like a large rodent, the feet belie this. The front feet have five widespread toes with large, sharp claws, good for grasping branches and characteristic of animals who catch live prey, similar to weasels. Herbivorous rodents, such as mice and squirrels, have only four toes on the front feet, effective for holding inert plant materials. The opossum back foot is unique: while it has three parallel middle toes, much like rodents, the pinky toe and thumb are opposable and the thumb has a large bulbous end but no claw, apparently aiding it in climbing branches.

It commonly walks in a two-by-two pace gait, similar to a raccoon, but often places its back foot directly on top of its front foot track. The two very differently shaped feet leave a confusing-looking track, toes sticking out in all directions. It is this chaotic look in itself that is diagnostic for this animal's track identification.

It scuttles through underbrush and thickets—and down our streets and culverts, having adapted well to suburban environments—in a slow trot or walk, giving it that bumbling appearance. But when tasked, it can undertake surprising bursts of speed, both on the ground and in the branches. It is also a proficient swimmer, employing its tail as a sculling oar.

The opossum has a popular reputation for dimwittedness, perhaps for having been slow to adapt to new developments like hunters with dogs, guns, traps, and its number one killer, the automobile. But this reputation flies in the face of its ability to have survived as a species for so long and illustrates the problem with trying to apply concepts of human intelligence to animals. In our arrogance, we rate animal intelligence in comparison to our obvious excellence at manipulating our environment, yet here we stand, a primate with barely a million years under our belt, facing, yet ignoring, our own probable extinction due to a lack of self-limiting behavior and a pathological urge to dominate.

The opossum, on the other hand, survives with a much more subtle set of strategies. First of all, it is extremely aware, despite its bumbling look. In the natural world, animals—birds in particular—are constantly talking with each other, spreading the news of what is going on around them, especially notifying each other of threats from predators. It is my sense that the opossum is a master of this kind of awareness, with its ancient history, and is an expert at simply avoiding trouble. And in its own frame of reference, it is quite intelligent: captive studies have shown that it has a remarkable memory for food sources. As it makes its rounds over a large territory, it files those locations for quick access when it circles back through. In addition, it has a very high intelligence for finding its way through mazes, more so than cats or dogs, a perfect skill for its underbrush habitat.

It has several related strategies that support its pacifist attitude. With its foraging habit, it is constantly on the move, rarely sleeping in the same spot for more than a day or two, appropriating any handy niche or burrow it finds for its bed, and simply gathering available debris for insulation. Thus, predators are never able to home in on it. Being a marsupial helps here too—the opossum is itself a moving den. The kids come along for the ride, at first in the marsupial pouch, where they nurse until fully developed as youngsters, then they do indeed crawl up on the back of their mother and go along for the ride until they are ready to move off on their own. Finally, they are fastidiously clean and nearly odorless, making it particularly difficult for a scent-hunter, such as a coyote, to find them.

This is contrary to their common reputation for being smelly and repulsive, which turns out to be yet another brilliant deception. Their survival strategy of last resort is to play dead. This is not a myth. When actually cornered and under attack, they use this final ploy, but they don't just stop at falling over and going limp. They actually enter a semi-catatonic state. They completely check out and may not come to for hours. Along with collapsing onto their sides, their lips curl up to show those alarming teeth, they emit foam from their mouth and nostrils, and secrete a foul-smelling fluid from anal glands, all a beautifully choreographed dance of qualities that are highly effective in a dangerous situation.

Related to all of this is their exceptional immunity to tick bites and Lyme disease, as well as to snake bites and rabies. These are qualities that are being researched in the hopes of finding applications in treating humans.

Despite all of their deceptions—the teeth, the odd-looking large head, the coarse-looking fur, the defensive smell—as pets they are known to be quite sweet, soft, friendly, and rarely ever provoked to bite. This is an animal who has used its long time on earth to great personal advantage, for adaptation rather than domination. Here is an animal who perhaps has something we can learn from, a hero in its own right. Couldn't we all be a little better at avoiding trouble and confrontation, simply minding our own business and getting better at what we do?

October 2018

The Dog Days: August and September

Out in the wilds of West Marin, it really is the dog days of summer. Foxes and coyotes are enjoying an abundance of prey, and, judging by sightings and tracks, their litters of young were very successful. This was the first year I have ever seen coyote pups out by themselves, and this month I saw two of them in different parts of the park. There is something undeniably cute about a half-sized, long-limbed, fuzzy young coyote!

Both sightings were mid-morning, possibly indicating that the pups hadn't quite mastered the art of nighttime hunting or the surreptitious nature of adults. But those super-intelligent canines are quite unfazed by human presence. They can clearly differentiate between hunters and hikers and don't make terribly big efforts to hide when they don't need to. A sighting, in itself, can be an expression of coyote well-being and comfort. In addition, fox and coyote scats, scattered across our landscapes in great abundance, testify to their wide use of open space and to the corresponding abundance of food, from rodents and rabbits to orchard fruits and road kill.

Though I never see foxes on my own bluff-edge property, I have heard many tales this year of clutches of gray fox pups cavorting in other yards, denning under decks and in close-by thickets. Foxes find safety from coyotes, who will kill them, given a chance, by hugging territory under the protective umbrella of human habitation. That and their clear preference for forest thickets make for a workable arrangement with the coyotes, who strongly favor open habitat where they can run unrestricted.

While both dog species enjoy fall fruit crops, foxes include a much higher proportion of fruit in the regular diet, commensurate with their forest habitat. Their scats are always an interesting story, telling of their movements and food availability. Examining their artfully placed scats for berry content proves to be a great indicator of the earliest huckleberries, usually a month or two before I begin finding them myself. The berry content of fox scats reveals the history and succession of local wild berry ripening cycles: from huckleberries to blackberries to wax myrtle, manzanita and salal. The gray fox is unique in how clearly differentiated its rodents meals and fruit meals are, the two rarely mixed in their pellet-shaped scats the way they are in twisty coyote scats.

This is another reason why, in the dog days of summer, our wild canines are thriving: they have an arrangement with the raccoons. When the raccoon families come in to strip one of our pear trees, so adept at harvesting them two or three days before we think they are ready, the foxes join in the party. While the gray fox is a good climber, the raccoons are better; the foxes are happy to be part of the cleanup crew, the job often taking only a night or two. There is almost always a raccoon scat latrine near these fruit tree raids, with a few scats full of the shells of their other favorite food—creek-side crustaceans, crabs and crawdads—making identification easy. But up on some raised object in the vicinity, you will find fox pellets, too.

Meanwhile, out on our shorelines, tracks and scat reveal another aspect of summer abundance, so counter-intuitive to the drought gripping the state. Actually, the coastal climate has been very beneficial for plant growth this year—the summer has been warm, and the fogs have been heavy and wet, a great combination. One coastal plant in particular, the sea rocket (a low-impact non-native), with fleshy foliage and seed pods shaped like Flash Gordon rocket ships, has been exceptionally prolific. The seedpods are favored by deer mice in the foredunes. Under the plants, in pockets in the sand, are large drifts of seedpods opened on one side with visible mouse tooth marks, the seeds removed. This plant by itself may be responsible for the booming seashore mouse populations.

In similar locations, brush rabbits are also having explosive population growth this year, partly fueled by the sea rocket crops. The rabbits prefer the succulent foliage, in many cases stripping the plants bare. Rabbits tend to go through population cycles that are more extreme than other mammals, and this is the year for our little cottontails. In some places, the foredunes are covered with their tracks and trails, extensive rabbit highways and broad social "party zones" where they congregate at night, in concentrations far greater than anything I have ever seen.

I watched the jackrabbit population go through a similar boom, and then a bust, when the drought began a few years ago. I suspect that the jackrabbit crash, in turn, had something to do with the disappearance of the coyote families who had crisscrossed the basin regularly for years. It was only after a two-year absence of coyotes in the basin that one female finally returned this year and laid claim to the territory, possibly the first one to take advantage of the renewed mouse and brush rabbit presence. Now, slowly, with the expanding brush rabbit territories, coyotes are returning to old patterns, but the jackrabbits have yet to return. Taking a guess, I would expect this winter to be particularly successful for canine reproduction and that we'll be seeing more of them next spring.

With this abundance of small prey, our bobcats will also do very well, so perhaps we can call this the cat days of summer too.

September 2013

Walking in the Dark

When I was a child, I was afraid of the dark, like most kids who aren't carefully introduced to the night. I was terrified of the imaginary wolves that lived behind the house, ready to attack me when I took the trash out on winter nights. I'd turn on every light I could find that would illuminate the route and then run as fast as I could. It was a convincing fear. Luckily, those wolves never ate me, and I loved being outside so much that I soon outgrew my unease.

I began running through the hills late into the summer nights. I came to thoroughly enjoy being outside in the dark. I learned that there was nothing to be afraid of out there. Instead, I became familiar with the nighttime landscapes and how to move in them with limited vision. But there was still a lot of mystery in the darkness and so much I didn't know about the nocturnal life of animals. With no mentors—my parents and teachers were just as unfamiliar with nature in darkness as I was—it was a slow learning process, but my comfort level grew steadily with knowledge and experience. I learned to love those moments, and to this day I enjoy hiking into the dusk and returning after dark, or going out early in the morning before light to experience dawn in wilder settings. These crepuscular times can yield surprising animal sightings, always a gift worth the trouble.

I walked out to the coast well before dawn one moonless night, navigating by the feel of the ground as much as anything else. I reached an extensive area of sandy hummocks and began slowly and methodically working my way through the terrain, becoming quieter and more blended with each step.

At the first sign of light, I caught a glimpse of a coyote toward the west, but she spied me first and quickly disappeared behind a dune. Always eager to study the tracks of an animal I've just seen, I went over to where I last saw her and found her prints. This is how the Apaches learned so much about tracks—by watching the movements of animals they could easily see in the open desert landscapes and directly relating that movement to the details in the tracks they found. I wanted to see the tracks of her turn-away and then see if I could follow her trail. I became engrossed in these tracks and followed them for a short distance, carefully reading the nuances of movement they reflected. Meanwhile, she had circled around and suddenly popped up at the top of a dune to the east, just as the sun rose behind her, bathing her exquisite fur in a brilliant rosy halo. She stared down at me for a moment, radiant, healthy, beautiful. In a blink she was gone again. I stood in awe, such an experience well worth the walk in the dark.

I've always thought it strange how the shift from dusk into dark seems to take so long, while the shift at dawn, from dark to light, seems so brief. In both cases, the darkness is a magical time to be out, but requires a sensory shift to negotiate.

The other night, I walked up the heavily wooded trail to a meadow at dusk and strolled back down in the dark, with just a sliver of a moon, to observe how I make that shift, how my senses change out of vision-oriented awareness to the many other layers of sensory orientation.

The first thing to realize and appreciate is that it is rarely really dark. Even on a moonless night, there is a great deal of ambient light from simple starlight, even when filtered through our coastal fog. Though full night vision can take half an hour to develop, our eyes do adjust, our brains calibrating to diminishing information. But night vision includes far more than sight.

First, there is that old primal fear to deal with. Perhaps it is only with accumulated experience that we can become truly comfortable in the dark. The rational mind is a useful tool in this instance, telling us what we already know, that there is really nothing to fear, at least not in our present landscape. How dangerous is a deer or bobcat, who can hear and see you—and leave—long before you know they are there?

This is where knowledge helps, simply having more accurate information about which animals are likely to be out at night in any particular landscape and what threat they actually represent. The general rule is that they are far more afraid of you than you of them, and with very good justification. But animals are not supermen and can easily be surprised when they are preoccupied and going about their business. When startled, they can put up a show of bravado and threat. Backing off carefully usually takes care of the situation.

Once you adjust to darkness, it feels womblike—a familiar and comforting place. We can hide in the dark as easily as those imaginary wolves out by my trashcans. As a kid, when we'd play hide and seek in the dark, I learned that I could hide right under the noses of searchers who are blinded by their own flashlights. Darkness can teach us a great deal about ourselves if we pay attention, if we notice where our irrational fears begin to rise and learn how to deal with them.

Instead of groping in the dark, like most of us do, out of balance and stumbling around, arms outstretched, panicked, lost, and disoriented—in the woods, in our living rooms, and even in many of our relationships—we can consciously make a shift into the tracker mind. We can return to ourselves. Whether normal nighttime darkness, human psychological darkness, or simple daytime stress and confusion, we have a basic tactic: slow down. Then slow down a little more and breathe long, deep, rhythmic breaths. Come back into balance and awareness. Lighten up! Feel the ground underfoot. Listen deeply. Pay attention. Look around and see where you are.

The next thing is to relax. When we stand upright, drop our hands, steady ourselves, and begin to notice what the darkness has to tell us, we can embrace it, love it, and listen to its story, expecting the unexpected and responding fluidly. We begin to open all of our senses, using sound, smell, the feel of our skin, the sense of the ground, and the slightest glimmers of reflected light to map our surroundings. With these simple shifts, we can reorient ourselves and begin to remember that we are in familiar territory, the same as daytime, even in those few spots where we can't see a darn thing. It is still the same earth, and we have good mental maps to draw upon. Our other senses are designed to compensate for diminished vision. It is another aspect of our evolutionary heritage.

Once we do this, it is as if a different light begins to glow in the landscape. In fact, shifting out of our sight-oriented view of the world and into the full spectrum of senses creates a much deeper sense of the world around us. The darkness awakens and comes to life. Once we begin to embrace darkness and befriend it, it is comical how obnoxious and undesirable a flashlight can be, as it instantly destroys that carefully won night vision and narrows the world down to a small, fearful circle. The key, as always, is slowing down and breaking out of habitual patterns, letting the world come to us instead of rushing through it.

In a couple of my classes with Tom Brown in the Pine Barrens years ago, we did a "Blindfold Drum Stalk," hiking out a couple of miles from the camp late at night, putting on a blindfold, and working our way back through the woods and the thickets toward a loud drum that was being beaten back at camp. I'd start out moving fearfully in that groping posture, completely blind and out of balance with no sense of the landscape.

Soon, though, I'd begin recovering my balance and start to get a feel for the shape of the ground and the sounds of the echoes. My senses would expand and I'd relax, loosen up, and start moving more fluidly and confidently. Once tuned in like this, I began to cut along quite quickly and easily, almost forgetting I couldn't see. Shifting to my remaining senses filled in the gaps of my absent vision. I discovered that my mental image of my surroundings, my instinctive mapping, did not depend on vision, and that my other senses very quickly stepped up to fill in the picture.

Sight was not essential! I really did understand the landscape and how to move through it. And as I calmed down, I quickly began tapping into a latent capacity for echo-location and mapping, filling in a three-dimensional awareness with this almost unconscious sense. In that relaxed state, I repeatedly found myself stopping for no apparent reason, only to reach out my hand to find a tree right in front of me that I might have bumped into, or, testing with my foot, a ditch one step away.

Was I unconsciously reacting to echoes or slight changes in the slope, or was something else going on, some awareness on a different level? It is hard to say, but after a while, walking blindfolded through the woods and thickets seemed as easy and relaxing as a walk in full daylight. This kind of experience becomes deeply satisfying, almost intoxicating. It is an experience of tapping into a deep sense of connection with the world that our usually busy minds often overlook. Primal instincts rise. We do know how to do this! We always did. A great sense of self-confidence floods our sense of being. The warrior spirit returns. We find a delight in striding along in the dark with a sense of confidence and good balance.

This applies to all aspects of life and to the unknowns we face on a daily basis. It is our fear that makes us move too fast and trip over obstacles. Learning to stop now and then, listening into the dark, the unknown, and facing it squarely can turn it into a true adventure, sensuous and enjoyable. Going just a bit further, it becomes possible, especially in the night, to connect with a level of awareness beyond the physical senses. This world speaks to us when we listen. It is our inner voice, our inner wisdom. What is there really to be afraid of? Most of it is in our imagination. When we calm ourselves, look around, and start asking questions, inner allies—our protectors—arise and walk along with us.

June 2010

The Journey and the Destination

As the year circles around, the shortening days, the longer nights, and the new chill in the mornings remind us that fall has arrived and winter is just around the corner. It evokes contemplative moods and occasional feelings of wistfulness as another year ends. Philosophy season is coming upon us! At our last tracking club meeting we used a quote from Tom Brown's Apache mentor, Stalking Wolf, as a guiding principle.

> *Most of the time, the journey is as important as the destination.*
> *Many times, the journey is more important than the destination.*
> *But often, the journey is the destination.*

Tom elaborated, telling the group, "Always assume that the journey is the destination; this will keep you safe. Always be ready to abandon or change the destination. Like a personal vision, it is always changing and evolving. In fact, destinations don't really exist; they are always re-forming with each choice we make."

The lessons of tracking and awareness are often the lessons of life, but in this regard, particularly so. It is provocative to ask: How much time in the outdoors do we spend "untracking," and similarly, how much time in our life do we waste un-living? The real journey is to live each moment, to savor it before it is gone, before we are gone, and to pass this savoring on to our children and grandchildren.

The responsibilities of life are destination points. The things we love to do, and the clarity of purpose we seek, are destination points. But these things have no true end. There is never a final destination where you say: "I've made it, I'm done." This is illusory. There is always another step behind it. It circles back around. The destination is truly the present. It is an endless journey. We are guided forward by our spirit and our dreams, but each step on the journey is the actual destination.

If each step is truly felt, fully lived, invested with passion and the fire of life, it is a complete step, and the next step becomes clear. To live is a journey. To eat and maintain a nest is a journey. What is the destination then? It is to live each of these moments of life. What destination can there be other than to make it a good journey? I have never been afraid of death when I am satisfied that I am living. When I am truly living, each moment is a complete eternity.

It is easy to drift away from this, to lose track in our haste, but that is always counterproductive and leads down a road to disappointment. Instead, as tracking constantly teaches, the art of life is to make each step, each breath, each word, and each action a sacred prayer, a purpose in itself. In this way it is a meditation, but not in the sense of a practice separate from life. It is the meditation of living.

When this way of living is firmly established, the discordant notes of destination desperation—tight focus, body tensing, irritation, and impatience—all feel obvious, loud and out of place. It doesn't feel good. That means such feelings can be usefully employed as a trigger reminding us to *stop*, relax, and return to aliveness. This holds true whether it is a project we are trying to complete before the end of the day or a major life plan. The truth of this can often be seen in immediate validations when we make that choice. The opportunities are everywhere.

On a recent tracking club outing, we discussed some of these ideas in our opening circle before starting down the trail. Having let go of destinations for a while, we began our walk with no plan other than to be in the moment and see what we could find. Immediately, we spied an animal nearly a mile away, moving across the plowed fields. By its general posture, its arched back and choppy trot, we could tell that it was a coyote.

While we watched, it trotted steadily, but when it got about fifty yards from the fence line, that coyote suddenly took off like a bolt of lightning! It turned into a flash of color, flickering light and dark as it flew through the scattered stands of brush, heading toward the pine thicket on the shore of the lagoon. Our jaws collectively dropped. That coyote was moving! We had no idea a coyote could run that fast. No wonder they can catch jackrabbits! In a blink of an eye it had crossed the slope and disappeared into the pines. We stood in wonderment, replaying what we had just seen.

What spurred the coyote into that burst? We certainly got a glimpse of its long-distance awareness, but was it just reacting to us? We were, after all, trackers, a relatively low-key bunch. There was indeed more to it, and later we found out what had happened.

The distant coyote, heading toward water and cover, was working an angle of travel that accounted for our group, even so far away. But its plan shifted when two things happened at once. A trail crew arriving behind us was just parking and unloading with a clang of shovels and a flash of orange jumpsuits. In the other direction, invisible to us at the time, a returning hiker, whose approach had been masked by the noise of the wind and distant surf, had rounded a corner in the trail and surprised the coyote. The coyote reacted to the situation by taking a fast shot through, from its perspective, a narrowing gap, before it was too late. Once it got its speed up, it simply kept going. Even at that distance I had a feeling that it enjoyed its speed and kept running purely because it felt good.

The lesson was taken, and for the next two hours, we stayed firmly rooted to exactly where we were in each moment, letting the earth surprise us, pulling one beautiful story after another out of the land, accepting these stories as they were offered to us.

I think Grandfather and Tom were right. I watch this unfold every day. I found myself struggling just yesterday, doing chores at home. The afternoon was moving along, and my goal was to fix a fence where cattle were getting through. That involved fixing a gate that was getting jammed. I felt tired and the wind was biting. I wasn't enjoying myself at all, just pushing to get the task done, grouchy because it looked like it would take the rest of the day. Every step was a push.

But I rebelled at that grouchy feeling. I remembered the principle of the journey and reclaimed myself. I had a different project that I was more interested in, at a warmer spot around the house. I let go of the destination I had locked onto; it could wait. Heck with the cows! I got involved in the new project and began enjoying the activity and the beautiful afternoon, completely released from the compulsion to finish anything.

Before I knew it, I found myself back at the fence in a completely different state of mind. I had a new plan for how to proceed. The rest of the project took but a few minutes. The wind, so oppressive before, was now just a pleasant cooling breeze. The journey had brought me back around, all on its own, to the destination.

November 2011

Super Vision

Each year for the last fifty years, I have spent at least a couple of weeks wandering around in the most remote corners I can find in the High Sierras. It feeds my soul. Those trips make my whole year work better. Up there, in the stony recesses of glacial-carved granite basins and ridges, I touch the infinite, the source of life. The hard work required to get there keeps me on a path of healthy habits all year long. You could say that those brief moments in the far reaches of glacial cirques organize my entire life.

The quality of my experience in the mountains is how I define the term "wilderness." From the moment I leave the car and the road, I feel like I'm returning to something—to a part of myself, to a sense of walking free in a healthy world. I'm returning to a legacy that I've inherited, to a spectacularly beautiful part of the earth that is being held in public trust, unscathed by modern industry. Once I leave the hiking trails and begin navigating across open landscapes, I remember where I have come from and I feel the land, pristine and untrammeled by man, cleansing my mind and soul. I walk through a world of sky and rock and tumbling streams.

Those clear-running streams seem to flow through me: I become a clear-running stream. To walk through a place where nature is protected and defended instead of extracted and degraded, brings a song to my heart and wings to my feet. I'm freed, and I know this is an old truth. The miles pass easily through those alpine meadows and over rocky passes, over waves of granite ridges tossed by geologic time like stormy seas, through boulder fields that must be carefully crossed, and along the exquisite mossy streams that splash their way down the canyons. The wind, the stone, the arching sky, the fragile meadows, they speak for themselves here, and they are sufficient.

I was lucky enough recently to spend a week backpacking in remote Kings Canyon high country, in the Sierra Nevada. After five days without seeing another human, crossing challenging passes and wandering off trail through vast and seldom-traveled granite basins, in a pristine landscape almost solely composed of rock and sky, I was fully immersed in the moment. I had wandered up into an isolated wrinkle far from the trails, a fairytale world of tiny lakes dotted with bright granite islands and picturesque clumps of stunted white bark pines, like a Chinese landscape painting. It had rained a little the evening before, but the morning had broken clear, the air sparkly clean and bright, with billowy white clouds signaling the end of the storms. The meadows were bright green, and the edges of the ponds were lined with thick emerald carpets of glowing, recharged mosses.

I had a long morning of ease ahead. I wandered around, soaking up the scene. My mind had quieted into an embracement, if you will, of the present moment, at one with the world, timeless and unhurried. I was simply strolling along when my vision abruptly shifted, and suddenly my sight turned into what I can only call super vision.

Everything came into extremely sharp focus, yet my awareness was deeply three-dimensional and panoramic, almost as if I were seeing from multiple angles at once, as if I had just stepped into a cubist painting. My sweeping glance at the ground revealed every pine needle and pebble in exquisitely sharp detail, with intense color and depth. Sounds intensified. The air tingled, and my skin vibrated with sensitivity. The coolness of the air on my shady side contrasted with the warmth of the morning sun on my sunny side. Even the topography seemed enhanced, almost exaggerated. Everything was heightened. Greens and blues, greys and browns: colors grew vividly pigmented, infinitely shaded. It was wonderfully quiet up there in the granite landscape, but distant Clark's Nutcracker calls pierced the air, and the slight whisper of the light breeze through the pine boughs grew louder. It was shocking. It hit like a bolt.

In tracking we call this "popping," when our minds reach a certain state and track details start jumping out of the ground. It was a remarkable moment, and thanks to years of tracking, I knew how to hold that state, enjoying it without disrupting it, breathing steadily, staying calm, and simply letting it roll: a sacred time. I wandered like that for hours, feeling as if I had stepped into a different world, soaking it all in, the beauty exquisite in every detail. It had taken a firm hold. A few days of deep wilderness will do this! Finally, in the early afternoon, when I had started picking my way down the talus slopes on the way out, I began returning to sensory normality. A feeling of inner peace remained with me long into the day.

I love those wild mountains, but I can find a similar state of wildness within minutes of my backyard: we have a wilderness at out fingertips. Life is healthy and abundant in our national seashore. Diversity, the fundamental sign of ecological health, is high. There are a few areas where monoculture and degradation still reign, but even those are slowly changing with the help of restoration programs and sustainable rangeland management. There are no mines or logging operations, no sprawling development, no shopping malls. Human impact and pollution are being carefully managed. The trajectory is forward. Health is returning here after coming dangerously close to the edge of the cliff of the typical extract, develop, and pollute cycle wherever modern industrial society reaches.

This is all it takes. This is Wilderness: a land that is tended and healthy, managed for its wildness, for what we can give rather than what we can take. The Point Reyes seashore is a world-class jewel. There is very little concentrated and untrammeled land of such spectacular beauty, fecundity, diversity, and scope of habitat anywhere in the world, and much of what exists is under relentless attack from our ever-more voracious species. Wild, non-industrialized land preserves, particularly an estuarine one like Point Reyes, are incredibly important for the future of humanity and the earth. This truth lies far beyond personal interests, such as whether or not I get to walk on unspoiled public beaches, hike in quiet woodlands, or dine on local oysters, whatever each of us thinks the land owes us. Lands like this offer us gifts far more valuable than the natural resources they contain. They offer us the possibility of personal insight and wisdom, of new ways to perceive the world.

More and more I find myself slipping into that mode of perception when I'm anywhere outdoors: I allow my eyes to scan the distant vistas, searching for the smallest details I can see, zeroing in on them with telescopic focus. Then I smoothly pull back into very close vision, focusing tightly on the smallest details right at hand. By ratcheting back and forth between these extremes, while taking in everything in between, the landscape comes to life, and underlying patterns appear.

Applying tracker knowledge to this intense level of awareness opens up a landscape in a way that compares to nothing else. Every little sign of animal activity feeds the picture: a nibbled leaf here, a scatter of fresh-dug soil there. The visual richness stimulates my other senses. Our minds are very visually oriented, but by pushing our usual visual limits, we free our other senses from their habitual constraints as well.

Seeing the world this way is intoxicating and liberating. The earth speaks. My eyes and ears drink up the patterns of the foliage and the topography, from meadows to thickets, which tell rich stories about the land and the weather. The richness of nearby detail gives context and perspective to the larger picture. The sounds and movements of birds fit into the patterns, both a manifestation of what is and a predictor of what will come. Animal trails begin telling their own stories: where they emerge, where they wander.

What I love most about this practice is how it can turn the most familiar and potentially boring walk into an exciting adventure. When I move into this perspective, a walk I've taken hundreds of times, such as the Bear Valley Trail or even the stroll across my yard, can come to life in new and ever-changing ways.

The surest way to stimulate this shift is simply to look farther and focus more tightly on distant details. Even after a lifetime spent in nature, I'm still teaching my mind to break through old limitations. I'm still amazed at how much more I can see, if I choose to. Now the flick of a deer's ear, for instance, in chaparral hundreds of yards away, will catch my attention. This might lead me to notice the activity of sparrows in those distant shrubs, then the hawk, silent and hidden in the branches of a tree. The subtle symphony of bird calls from that direction grows louder and starts to make sense in the current time and conditions. I begin to understand what they are talking about. Through this simple shift, I've quickly expanded my sphere of awareness, giving context and sharpness to closer surroundings.

As my eyes return from those distant details to focused close-up views, I nevertheless maintain an unfocused perspective, holding the entire landscape in my attention. It is a remarkable awareness process, so satisfying and delicious that it is easy to stay immersed. To my mind, this is contradictory and has taken years to learn, but in experience it is natural to do and readily available. I'm touching the animal within, genetic codes, embedded memories from eons past.

When I walk in our local forest landscapes this way, through the complex of oaks, firs, sword ferns, and hazelnut trees, it feels old, and I sense the hundreds of generations of Miwok people who, not long ago, wandered deer trails on these same slopes. I feel the same gladness and ease of beautiful summer days—days that felt endless then just as they do now. Deep in the wooded canyons, as I wander in a state of super vision, among trees whose ancestors go back far—who knows how long?—I hear the echoes of those ancient times, and they reach out and touch me, bridging the divide.

May 2016

Further Reading

Brown Jr., Tom, and William Watkins. *The Tracker: The Story of Tom Brown, Jr.* New York, NY: Berkley Books, 1985.

Brown Jr., Tom. *Awakening Spirits.* New York, NY: Berkley Books, 1994.

Brown Jr., Tom, Brandt Morgan, and Heather Bolyn. *Tom Brown's Field Guide—Nature Observation and Tracking.* New York, NY: Berkley Books, 1998.

Brown Jr., Tom. *The Science and Art of Tracking.* New York, NY: Berkley Books, 1999.

Elbroch, Mark, Eleanor Marks, and C. Diane Boretos. *Bird Tracks & Sign: A Guide to North American Species.* Mechanicsburg, PA: Stackpole Books, 2001.

Elbroch, Mark. *Mammal Tracks & Sign: A Guide to North American Species.* Mechanicsburg, PA: Stackpole Books, 2003.

Elbroch, Mark, and Kurt Rinehart. *Behavior of North American Mammals.* Boston, MA: Houghton Mifflin Harcourt, 2011.

Elbroch, Mark, Jonah Evans, and Michael Kresky. *Field Guide to Animal Tracks and Scat of California.* Berkeley, CA: University of California Press, 2012.

Lowery, James C. *The Tracker's Field Guide: A Comprehensive Handbook for Animal Tracking.* Guilford, CT: Falcon Guides, an Imprint of Globe Pequot Press, 2013.

Moskowitz, David. *Wildlife of the Pacific Northwest: Tracking and Identifying Mammals, Birds, Reptiles, Amphibians, and Invertebrates.* Portland, OR: Timber Press, 2010.

Rezendes, Paul. *Tracking and the Art of Seeing: How to Read Animal Tracks and Sign.* New York, NY: Quill/HarperCollins, 1999.

About Richard Vacha

Richard Vacha is the founder of the Marin Tracking Club and the Point Reyes Tracking School. He has been practicing animal tracking for three decades and has a class III certification through the international CyberTracker Tracker Evaluation program. He maintains a cabinetmaking and woodworking business from his home in Point Reyes Station, CA.

About Kayta Plescia

Kayta Plescia lives in Sebastopol, CA where she makes art and farms alongside her partner at Green Valley Community Farm.